SO-AIA-262

PROPERTY OF
HIGH POINT PUBLIC LIBRARY
HIGH POINT, NORTH CAROLINA

PRAISE FOR
Death to the BCS

"The most thoroughly researched, reasoned, and readable argument to date for college football reform." —*Time*

"The plan put forward by Wetzel, Peter, and Passan is certainly the strongest BCS-alternative to date. It is imperative that other sports journalists, college administrators, and football fans read *Death to the BCS*." —Brian Frederick, *The Huffington Post*

"Alternately brilliant and scary. You will put the book down sweaty, angry, and wishing you could do something to change the system." —Nando DiFino, *The Wall Street Journal*

"Required reading for college football fans." —Tony "Mr. College Football" Barnhart, *The Atlanta Journal-Constitution*

"What the book lacks in subtlety it makes up for in ferocity, attacking the BCS from the opening page and never letting up on the theme that the college football bowl system is a terrible way to crown a champion of a great sport." —Pat Forde, ESPN.com

"A love letter to logic, meticulously reported and written with the kind of clarity you suspect a preacher aspires to when trolling for possible converts." —Mike Vaccaro, *New York Post*

"This here is a rant, a metal chair to the head, a no-holds barred, no-mercy, none-dare-call-it-treason tirade. . . . It certainly makes the book a lot of fun to read and as irresistible as a caged match." —Joe Posnanski, SI.com

"I did not fully appreciate the folly of the BCS until I read *Death to the BCS*. There is damning material here."

—Michael Rosenberg, *Detroit Free Press*

"You might say the only positive thing the BCS has created in its history is this book."

—Matt James, *The Fresno Bee*

"As scornful as its title."

—Steve Wieberg and Jack Carey, *USA Today*

"The authors offer a compelling alternative plan."

—Matthew Ott, *Associated Press*

"The buzz of college football. The new book takes out the Bowl Championship Series at the knees."

—Dennis Dodd, CBS Sports

"It does grave damage to all the myths the BCS pushers spread like fertilizer, using a blend of facts, figures, interviews, anecdotes, and alternatives that confirm everything you ever presumed was wrong with college football's postseason. It gives hope that common sense will finally reign."

—Scott Michaux, *Augusta Chronicle*

"The playoff they've developed, a 16-team extravaganza that features home games for the top seeds until the national final in some warm weather site, makes practical and financial sense. Death to the BCS! Where's my pitchfork?"

—Bob Kravitz, *The Indianapolis Star*

"From missed class time to how it would impact the regular season, the book takes every argument made against a playoff and blows it up with the force of a bazooka. Reading *Death to the BCS* was especially poignant for me."

—Dan Wolken, *The Commercial Appeal* (Memphis)

"If you care about college football, regardless of how you feel about the BCS, the book is worth your time. It's informative, provocative, entertaining, and unapologetic—by far the most complete argument against the BCS."　　　　—Sam Mellinger, *The Kansas City Star*

"The book accurately and diligently points out what people have known for years: The BCS is fundamentally flawed, at times a joke, and very controversial."　　　—Chris Dufresne, *Los Angeles Times*

"Chances are, come January, the BCS will be a hot topic and anyone with an opinion will have better read this book."
　　　　　　　　　—Michael Coffey, *Publishers Weekly*

"The book is so chilling in its exposure of the unseemly side of the bowl racket, that you will feel compelled to shower each week after perusing the BCS standings. It's that infuriating."
　　　　　　　　　—Sean Pendergast, *Houston Press*

"Rejoice, all ye college football playoff supporters. You have a voice."
　　　　　　　　　—Tom Shatel, *Omaha World-Herald*

"The book details how the corrupt bowl system is a boon for athletic directors, conference commissioners, and bowl executives—but a money loser for just about everyone else, including athletic departments."　　　　　　　—Brian Murphy, *Idaho Statesman*

"A compelling argument carefully and painstakingly laid out."
　　　　　　　　　—Dan Hinxman, *Reno Gazette-Journal*

"This book makes an awfully, awfully strong case."
　　　　　　　　　—Sean Keeler, *The Des Moines Register*

"The book likely will convert even the most ardent playoff opponent."
　　　　　　　　　—Paul Costanzo, *The Times Herald*

"If you are a fan of college football, this is a must-read—even if you like the bowl system. No, make that especially if you like the bowl system."   —Jerry Palm, CBS Sports

"Not only does it expose a lot of the hypocrisy in the cash-driven BCS hierarchy, it gets into how flawed math and corruption determine what teams go to the national title game."
                              —Tom Hoffarth, *Los Angeles Daily News*

"An attack on the BCS that will make the power six conference commissioners cringe and enrage college football fans across the country."
                              —R.J. Young, *The Oklahoma Daily*

"In great detail, it debunks every myth set forth in defense of the bowl system, exposes a plethora of hypocrisies and offers a saner, more practicable, and more profitable alternative."
                              —Michael Arace, *The Columbus Dispatch*

DEATH TO THE BCS

DEATH TO THE BCS

The Definitive Case Against the Bowl Championship Series

DAN WETZEL, JOSH PETER, AND JEFF PASSAN

2011 EDITION

Totally Revised and Updated

GOTHAM BOOKS

PROPERTY OF
HIGH POINT PUBLIC LIBRARY
HIGH POINT, NORTH CAROLINA

GOTHAM BOOKS
Published by Penguin Group (USA) Inc.
375 Hudson Street, New York, New York 10014, U.S.A.

Penguin Group (Canada), 90 Eglinton Avenue East, Suite 700, Toronto, Ontario M4P 2Y3, Canada (a division of Pearson Penguin Canada Inc.); Penguin Books Ltd, 80 Strand, London WC2R 0RL, England; Penguin Ireland, 25 St Stephen's Green, Dublin 2, Ireland (a division of Penguin Books Ltd); Penguin Group (Australia), 250 Camberwell Road, Camberwell, Victoria 3124, Australia (a division of Pearson Australia Group Pty Ltd); Penguin Books India Pvt Ltd, 11 Community Centre, Panchsheel Park, New Delhi—110 017, India; Penguin Group (NZ), 67 Apollo Drive, Rosedale, Auckland 0632, New Zealand (a division of Pearson New Zealand Ltd); Penguin Books (South Africa) (Pty) Ltd, 24 Sturdee Avenue, Rosebank, Johannesburg 2196, South Africa

Penguin Books Ltd, Registered Offices: 80 Strand, London WC2R 0RL, England

Published by Gotham Books, a member of Penguin Group (USA) Inc.

First printing, October 2011
10 9 8 7 6 5 4 3 2 1

Copyright © 2011 by Dan Wetzel, Josh Peter, Jeff Passan
All rights reserved

Gotham Books and the skyscraper logo are trademarks of Penguin Group (USA) Inc.

LIBRARY OF CONGRESS CATALOGING-IN-PUBLICATION DATA
Wetzel, Dan.
    Death to BCS / Dan Wetzel, Josh Peter, and Jeff Passan. — Totally rev. and updated.
      p. cm.
    Includes index.
    ISBN 978-1-592-40686-9
    1. Football—United States.   2. College sports—United States.   3. Bowl Championship Series.   4. BCS National Championship Game (Football game)   I. Peter, Josh.
II. Passan, Jeff.   III. Title.   IV. Title: Death to the Bowl Championship Series.
    GV959.W48 2011
    796.332'63—dc23   2011022650

Printed in the United States of America
Set in Apollo MT Std
Designed by Sabrina Bowers

Without limiting the rights under copyright reserved above, no part of this publication may be reproduced, stored in or introduced into a retrieval system, or transmitted, in any form, or by any means (electronic, mechanical, photocopying, recording, or otherwise), without the prior written permission of both the copyright owner and the above publisher of this book.

The scanning, uploading, and distribution of this book via the Internet or via any other means without the permission of the publisher is illegal and punishable by law. Please purchase only authorized electronic editions, and do not participate in or encourage electronic piracy of copyrighted materials. Your support of the author's rights is appreciated.

While the author has made every effort to provide accurate telephone numbers and Internet addresses at the time of publication, neither the publisher nor the author assumes any responsibility for errors, or for changes that occur after publication. Further, the publisher does not have any control over and does not assume any responsibility for author or third-party websites or their content.

To John Junker, for proving our first edition correct

796.33263 Wetzel c.1
Wetzel, Dan.
   Death to the BCS
            30519008864061

CONTENTS

PROLOGUE

About five months after the October 2010 release of the first edition of this book came another tome that perfectly illustrated why college football is stuck with the Bowl Championship Series. A retired Arizona Supreme Court justice, two former FBI agents, and a host of others put together the "Final Report" of the Fiesta Bowl's internal investigation into its corrupt spending habits. Despite dealing with just a single bowl game, it ran nearly one hundred pages longer than *Death to the BCS*.

Nothing validated our book so much as that report, which pulled the veil off Fiesta Bowl CEO John Junker's payola scheme that lavished his cronies with cash and graft and golf. After reading the report and stumbling upon revelation after revelation, each more stunning than the last, it became obvious to us: We needed to rewrite this book.

So two extra chapters and 15,000 new words later, here is *Death to the BCS: Totally Revised and Updated*, which not only gives a blow-by-blow inside the Fiesta Bowl scandal but chronicles the 2010 season, offers what-should-have-been playoff brackets for the last five years, and tries to answer so many of the questions we received from around the country.

Questions from people like from Steve Johnson in Wisconsin, who wrote: "What can the average fan do?" And Connie Long in Pennsylvania: "Where do I begin with my letter-writing campaign to overturn the BCS?" And Kevin Mallory in Florida: "I would like to help spread the word."

It's simple: Tell a friend. Explain just one thing. Maybe it's the exorbitant salaries for bowl game CEOs. Or how universities can lose millions of dollars attending games with the highest payouts. Perhaps it's that players actually want a playoff. Could be the silly polls and mathematically bankrupt computer systems. The easiest thing would be to talk about the Fiesta Bowl and how it stands for everything college football shouldn't.

Over the past year, we found a nation of college football players, coaches, fans, and, yes, many, many administrators who sought the same thing: the truth. The response, not just in the issuing of multiple printings of the original book or endless media appearances, was amazing.

The media changed the way they covered bowl games and began asking more pointed questions of decision makers. Athletic directors called thanking us, acknowledging they hadn't fully understood the entire system. Many swore change was coming, especially when a new generation of leadership assumes control.

University presidents digested information their conference commissioners wouldn't dare tell them. A governor's annual Christmas reading list included *Death to the BCS*. The book inspired Mark Cuban, owner of the NBA champion Dallas Mavericks, to form a company in hopes of staging his own college football playoff.

More important, we heard from people across the country. One man made a music video. Another named Bob Watson in California said he was boycotting all products from Frito-Lay, the title sponsor of the Fiesta Bowl. "This is not easy," he wrote. "I *love* Fritos and Cheetos."

After the Fiesta Bowl report, Junker was fired. All the people who took his gifts are still around. The only thing they have to fear is the public knowing the truth about the system they continue to defend. It keeps coming and coming and coming.

Here's our latest shot at exposing it.

DAN WETZEL, JOSH PETER, AND JEFF PASSAN
JUNE 2011

DEATH TO THE

TO THE

BCS

INTRODUCTION

The Cartel

For three years, we pored over thousands of pages of tax filings, university contracts, and congressional testimony. We criss-crossed the country interviewing the pertinent power players in college football, on and off the record. We filed scores of Free-dom of Information requests. We wanted to answer one ques-tion: Why is college football *really* saddled with the brain-dead Bowl Championship Series? We sought the truth, because tens of millions of fans deserve it.

We discovered an ocean of corruption: sophisticated scams, mind-numbing waste, naked political deals, and systemic spin-doctoring from the suits in charge and their well-paid public relations people to hide an ugly reality. While the sleaze should be enough to cause the death of the BCS, it's simply emblematic of a long battle best represented by two men. One stands for common sense and the possibilities the great game can offer. The other is about protecting the one-sided system that enriches and empowers the very few who led college football into this morass, even as it runs counter to their teams' competitive interests.

You've heard of the first. His name is Joe Paterno. He's the eighty-four-year-old icon who, after sixty-two seasons coaching at Penn State, the last forty-six as head coach, is as steadfast a proponent of a playoff as ever. He is us. He is you. He is every-one whose gag reflex is triggered at the mere thought of how college football crowns its national champion.

You might not have heard of the other. His name is Jim Delany. He's the sixty-three-year-old commissioner of Penn State's conference, the Big Ten. He is one of the most powerful people in college athletics. His influence far outweighs that of even the NCAA president, because Delany belongs to the group that hijacked college football and refuses to let go.

Paterno may be the king of the sport, but Delany is the ayatollah, speaking the word of God.

And that word is *no*.

No to a playoff. No to an extra championship game following the bowl season. No to any semblance of sanity in America's greatest spectator sport. No to anything but the loathsome, odious, reviled BCS.

For thirteen years, the BCS has decided the national champion at the highest level of college football, Division I-A. Two human polls and one group of computerized rankings combine to determine the two teams that play in the BCS national championship game. Other top-ranked teams go to the BCS-supported Rose Bowl, Sugar Bowl, Orange Bowl, and Fiesta Bowl. Delany helped conceive the BCS amid widespread skepticism. It's been a bigger disaster than anyone could have imagined. Its approval rating among fans polled by *Sports Illustrated* hovers around 10 percent. And yet Delany draws the following conclusion: "It's been incredibly successful."

For him and his cronies, sure. The BCS is a group of similar, private businesses that bands together in search of money and power, harming the public along the way. It gives off a wretched smell—that of a cartel. Just ask the twenty-one economists and antitrust experts who called it that in a 2011 letter to the United States Department of Justice. The DOJ is now exploring whether to take up an antitrust lawsuit against the BCS. Rather than jack up gas prices or cut off the oil supply like

OPEC can, the BCS power brokers control the postseason and the revenue it generates while pretending a playoff would put at risk something as sacred as the history and tradition of the Beef 'O' Brady's Bowl.

Officially, the BCS is run by twelve men: the commissioners of major college football's eleven conferences and the athletic director of Notre Dame. Realistically, six men control college football: the commissioners of the Atlantic Coast, Big East, Big Ten, Big 12, Pac-12, and Southeastern conferences. They squirrel away the sport's revenues, crush any challenge to their supremacy, and make decision after ill-fated decision that take college football eons further from what its fans want.

Alongside Delany, Mike Slive (SEC), Dan Beebe (Big 12), John Swofford (ACC), Larry Scott (Pac-12), and John Marinatto (Big East) guide the system to a place where their conferences receive automatic bids to the BCS games with massive payouts. This is college football's Cartel.

It exists to consolidate control among the power conferences and position them to never let go. Suggesting a playoff to the Cartel is futile because it doesn't care how big the postseason revenue pie gets or even if its slice would grow. It simply wants to ensure that no one else holds the knife.

The six Cartel members work with a legion of well-paid executive directors from a couple dozen bowl games and a few high-powered athletic directors and school presidents to dictate how the sport operates. Formally, the Cartel doesn't exist. Neither, for that matter, does the BCS. It's not a legal construct, just a series of contracts among various entities, which makes it hard for opponents to trace it, sue it, or pin it down. As much as government officials yearn to bust it using the Sherman Antitrust Act before the current BCS television deals run out in 2014 (in addition to the Justice Department's interest, the attorney general of Utah said he would file suit and encouraged other states to join him), the case is not a certain winner, even if the BCS seems so patently wrong.

The BCS says it exists to provide a title game between the two teams it deems best. Of course, anyone who's been paying attention to college football over the past decade would take issue with the BCS's success in determining that best teams. More than a dozen teams have finished the regular season undefeated and have been denied a spot in the BCS championship game. In truth, the BCS is far more than just a means to determine a true national champion. It's both a political power play and a way to protect private bowl interests at the expense of fairness, taxpayers, and college football fans.

"It has given the commissioners power and significance," said Gene Bleymaier, the former athletic director at Boise State University. "Prior to this, conference commissioners had very little power. No one knew them. They had very little significance outside of their conference."

Joe Paterno is too old to care about perceived power. He wants what's fair, and that is a playoff. Four times he led Penn State to undefeated seasons and didn't win a national championship. Perhaps no other person has been so wronged by the lack of a proper postseason. It may be the only issue where Paterno is considered a forward-thinking revolutionary. Paterno translated the *Aeneid* from Latin to English in high school and said the epic poem guides his coaching style. He claimed he has neither sent nor read an e-mail in his life. When the NCAA imposed legislation that limited coaches sending text messages to recruits, he was baffled.

"I thought it was tech messaging—T-E-C-H," Paterno told *The New York Times.*

Paterno knew how to use the phone, and one particular day

the lack of a playoff so aggravated him that he called Jim Delany. Paterno didn't hold back. The Cartel can make anything happen in college football, and even Paterno, a man who loathes change, understood college football needed it. Delany told Paterno that the university presidents with the power to change the system were pro-BCS. Paterno insisted that the presidents would follow wherever Delany led. Delany didn't budge. The call ended without resolution. Nothing would change.

The Cartel doesn't just laugh at Joe Paterno. It laughs at you, too. The joke is on fans who dream of college football finding a postseason worthy of its pageantry. Even the leader of the free world is beyond its reach. In November 2008, President-elect Barack Obama declared that the sport needed a playoff. Delany treated the president of the United States the same way he does every challenger to his monopoly: He dismissed him. "I think it's that time of year," he told Pete Thamel of *The New York Times*.

The Cartel entrenched itself through a campaign that spreads misinformation and perpetuates falsehoods. Debate about how to fix college football is ill-informed and often dizzies the participants. This is exactly how the powers that be want it. By shrouding the most important part of their sport in confusion and mystery, and by tossing out phony arguments and distracting canards, and even by having spokesmen obfuscate the facts in front of Congress, the Cartel has so waylaid college football that even a do-anything spirit like Joe Paterno throws his hands up in defeat.

Fortunately, we know a few things Paterno doesn't.

We know how the BCS really works, or, more accurately, doesn't work. It's every bit as troubling as the old coach can imagine. Because of the BCS, universities have blown almost $3 million paying for empty seats at a single game. Because of the BCS, athletic directors cash $50,000 bonus checks, even for sending teams to D-list bowl games, and during the off-season enjoy lavish gifts, golf weekends, and Caribbean cruises from bowl directors desperate to maintain their privileged setup. Because of the BCS, teams are rewarded for waltzing through cupcake schedules every fall. Because of the BCS, Division I-A college football is the only sport in which the NCAA declines to crown an official national champion.

There is no smoking gun with the BCS. The BCS *is* the smoking gun.

The BCS has corrupted and demeaned the bowl system, which is a terrible shame. We love the idea of bowl games. The major ones and the little ones, the unusual matchups, the crazy comebacks, the nothing-to-lose finishes. How the Independence Bowl in Shreveport, Louisiana, and the Sun Bowl in El Paso, Texas, still mean something to their communities. While critics cry about too many bowls, we disagree. More football is never a bad thing. The problem is how the business of bowl games prevents progress.

The power-conference commissioners scheme to protect their dominant position in the postseason. The bowl executives rake in huge salaries while serving as middlemen and publicly acknowledging their core business has nothing to do with honoring the sport. "We're not about college football," Gator Bowl president Rick Catlett told Jacksonville TV station WJXT in December 2010. "We're about economic impact."

The bowl system is the most illogical business arrangement in sports. The NCAA outsources its most important and profitable product, the college football postseason. Bowl games take a cut of up to 60 percent of gross revenue. More than 50 percent of universities participating in bowls spend more money than they receive. All so people who are "not about college football" can cash in on the millions.

The outdated bowl business blocks progress with its white-knuckle grip on the sport. Forget the month of football nirvana a playoff would provide. Today, the schools lose, the fans lose, and the sport itself loses. Doesn't matter, because the suits win, quite handsomely, and to defend the indefensible they resort to bad arguments, anything to quiet the constant din for a playoff.

"How would band members, cheerleaders, and other students make holiday plans knowing their team might play one, two, or three games on campus during the time they are normally home with their families?" BCS executive director Bill Hancock asked.

Inconvenienced cheerleaders are a prime defense for the BCS. Such rationale comes as much from hubris as foolhardiness. The BCS treats college football fans as if they're stupid. It takes credit for the rise in the sport's popularity, comparing today's title game to the mess of split championships that preceded it. It's like trying to say a busted calculator is good because it's newer than an abacus.

The system isn't merely broken, either. It is smashed, crushed, twisted, and mangled, totaled beyond belief, and there is no fixing it. College football needs to start over. Only the Cartel won't budge, not when it has the power, which, in this case, it deems more valuable than the additional cash a playoff would create.

And it's a lot of money. An awful lot. Experts estimate a college football playoff would gross at least $750 million in annual revenue, nearly tripling the current system. A panel of current and former television executives believe that the TV contract alone would bring in at least $450 million, a reasonable sum considering sports might be the last DVR-proof event. Ticket sales of more than $150 million, sponsorships adding another $120 million, and other miscellany, from merchandising to concessions, would provide college athletics with needed cash.

The old bowls would survive mostly as is, no matter what dire catastrophes the Cartel predicts. Run in concert with the playoff, they would generate another $100 million plus in gross revenues. As tuition rises to obscene levels, endowments dry up, donations plummet, and only 14 of 120 Division I-A schools turn a profit on their athletic departments, the BCS bosses continue to sit on a diamond mine because they so relish their position.

Without NCAA oversight and no impartial official looking out for the universities' welfare, the BCS honchos act like the worst of our politicians—more concerned with spending riders, petty pork projects, and special-interest groups than what's best for the nation. Among the Cartel there is a lack of comity and commonality, a stark contrast to its sport, which every Saturday beams with millions of people at historic on-campus stadiums sharing passion and memories and beer and the dream of a playoff.

A grassroots groundswell beyond governmental intervention threatens the establishment. Already Boise State, the University of Utah, and Texas Christian, upstart programs from smaller conferences, have penetrated the BCS and won major bowl games over big-name opponents. The victories only steeled the Cartel and prompted a new philosophy: If you can't beat 'em, invite 'em. Utah gained an invitation to the Pac-12 beginning in 2011 and TCU to the Big East in 2012.

The system, meanwhile, dared not change. Championship access means money, and money could turn the Boise States of the world into annual powerhouses. Soon enough, people might start asking why the six major conferences get to call the shots. They took 83.4 percent of the $174.1 million paid out by BCS games in 2011, while the Mountain West Conference, Western Athletic Conference, Mid-American Conference, Conference USA, and Sun

Belt Conference scraped by with the leftovers. The control of money, then, is sacrosanct, far more than the promise of underdogs slaying historic programs, of games in December and January climaxing with a real championship, of March Madness–level excitement in a football playoff.

So for now the BCS survives, a roach amid a typhoon of Raid. The unyielding push of common sense and the continued uncovering of corruption are held off with mistruths and misdirection that turn the entire issue into a river of red herrings.

Facts have power, though. The truth has might. The rational presentation of both can upend even the longest-held conventional wisdom and expose the Cartel for what it is: a not-half-as-smart-as-it-wants-you-to-believe group of leaders that history one day will mock for its obstinacy.

To properly dismantle the BCS, we need to start by defining a suitable alternative. An argument against something is hollow without a superior substitute. So before we get to the goriest details of everything wrong with the BCS, we'll take you through all that's right with our playoff plan, something that would stand on its own even without the BCS serving as a sham of a solution.

"The single most frustrating notion is, 'We understand it's not perfect, but it's the best we can do,'" Mountain West commissioner Craig Thompson said. "That's just irritating. There are a lot of smart people, creative people."

In seeking the optimal playoff plan, we did something the Cartel would never dare: We talked with those smart, creative people—conference commissioners, marketing professionals, athletic directors, television executives, economists, professors, bowl representatives, NFL executives, college players, and more. They brainstormed, hypothesized, planned, and ruminated, and together it came, an impermeable idea whose lone impediment is six men and the control they refuse to cede.

What follows is no fantasy, no wild theory, no pipe dream that's alive only in some heavenly place where Woody Hayes and Bear Bryant are coaching against each other. It's tangible and feasible, and it benefits every TV entity, every university, every player, every coach, and especially every fan.

This is what a real playoff looks like.

1 The Plan

There are three chief criteria for a playoff plan to work:

1. It must be more profitable in every imaginable way for colleges and universities.
2. It must protect, if not increase, the value of the regular season.
3. It must take academics into consideration, if only so presidents can save face for their long-standing hypocrisy on the issue.

The Cartel seems to want playoff proponents to argue about the right plan, because the greater the variety of proposals out there, the easier it is to dismiss them all as the confused ramblings of uninformed outsiders. They desire the devil to be in the details. Squabbling over specifics of the replacement model gives the BCS life, causing distraction and division and allowing the status quo to remain. And with tens of millions of angry fans, there is no shortage of ideas. Unfortunately, most are unworkable.

Nearly all of the plans out there are superior to the current setup, whether a four-team (also known as a "plus-one"), six-team, eight-team, twelve-team, or some other design. We'd take any of them over the BCS. We're open to compromise.

Some plans are more politically feasible than others. We prefer to reject being handcuffed by cronyism and weak leadership and instead believe in a bold, yet realistic, blow-it-up-and-start-from-scratch system. Our plan fixes the greatest problems while maintaining the most integrity. Even the staunchest Cartel members, such as former Pac-10 commissioner Tom Hansen, have said the model we use is the only acceptable option.

First, let's get rid of the nonstarters: Any plan that includes dropping regular-season games, eliminating conference championship games, realigning leagues, or using bowl games as host sites for playoff games would never pass muster. The Cartel knows as much. Those are exactly the kind of doomed plans it wants pushed forward.

Our plan for Division I-A football: a sixteen-team playoff that provides automatic bids for all eleven conference champions and at-large slots for five remaining teams. Yes, all eleven conference champions, even the lousy ones, determined through traditional means: either the regular season or conference title games, which would continue unabated. While no one would argue that the Sun Belt champ is one of the top sixteen teams in the country, its presence is paramount to maintaining the integrity and relevancy of the regular season. It creates incentive for regular-season success.

The best teams earn the highest seeds and are rewarded with home games for the first three rounds. The championship game is held at a neutral site. The No. 1 seed doesn't just get rewarded with the weakest opponent—in most years the Sun Belt champion—but the ensuing rounds on its home field. Finish fifth and face a first-round battle against a No. 12 seed likely from a power conference, then a second-round game on the road. The difference between first and fifth is significant.

By playing games on campus, the tournament also would include what is perhaps the best part of college football: its historic stadiums and game-day environments. There's no good reason to conduct playoff games before under-capacity crowds at sterile municipal stadiums in far-off cities when the incomparable feeling of the Swamp in Gainesville, the Horseshoe in Columbus, or the Coliseum in Los Angeles beckons. Suddenly, the top seeds' squaring off against small-conference competition doesn't lend itself to fan apathy. Devotees would pack their home stadiums, and television viewers would be treated to the Cinderella possibility college football so sorely lacks.

The men's basketball tournament is successful because in early games little schools dare to dream, and in the Final Four the deserving survivors duke it out for supremacy. That combination creates incredible drama, draws in casual fans, and delivers the television ratings that generated a fourteen-year, $11 billion TV contract. Perhaps the Mid-American Conference champion would never win a football playoff, but the possibility that a MAC team could—not to mention the likelihood that soon enough, a high seed will be upset in the first round—portends magic.

A twelve-person selection committee, similar to the one used for the men's basketball tournament, would determine the five at-large bids and seeding. After eliminating confused poll voters and mathematically dubious formulas from the equation, the selection committee would rely on a number of tools to inform its choices. Objective data from the best-performing computerized models that take into account margin of victory as well as subjective analyses from scouts and other football personnel who understand the game's nuances would provide a sufficient knowledge base. Teams that finish well would receive stronger consideration than those that faded. The committee would place particular emphasis on strength of schedule to encourage the best out-of-conference matchups. By loading the committee with big- and small-school ADs and conference commissioners, the representation would be fair and equal. Arguments over the final spots and seeding would happen just as they do with berths to BCS bowls, only they would center on which two-loss team was left out, not which unbeaten school missed its shot at the championship.

Any team, big or small, independent or affiliated, would be eligible for an at-large bid. Notre Dame, Brigham Young University, and the service academies could gain entry with one of the five at-large slots. Competition for them would make the final month of the regular season a circus of action, playoff chances coming and going with each touchdown, excitement saturating the country. It would compel Pac-12 fans to follow the Big East, SEC fans to pay attention to the Mountain West, ACC fans to study up on the Western Athletic Conference. TV ratings would jump. The Internet would buckle from excitement. A playoff wouldn't hurt the regular season, as the BCS claims.

"I don't understand how anybody could put that out there," longtime Texas athletic director DeLoss Dodds said. "It's the [opposite]. A playoff builds the season."

Even back in the mid-1990s an NCAA committee on football's postseason interviewed the presidents of all six major television entities and found a consensus: Television ratings and regular-season revenue for individual conferences would soar with even a small playoff.

It's actually the BCS that's adversely affecting the popularity and profitability of the regular season by keeping ratings below potential. The NFL has built itself into the most popular sport in America in part because of its annual postseason tournament, which builds the season up and carries over year to year.

"There is empirical evidence that leagues with playoffs receive a ratings increase. I don't think college football would be any different," said West Virginia athletic director Oliver Luck, who spent decades as a professional sports executive, including with the NFL, before returning to his alma mater in 2010. "If a [December] NFL game with playoff implications receives a bump in interest, I would take the view that the pattern for college football would be the same."

The entire playoff would be conducted over four weeks, the same time frame in which the current bowl schedule operates. The playoff would allow a two- to three-week break for final exams for student-athletes, then kick off the weekend before Christmas and conclude the second Monday of January. In 2011 and 2012, that's the same date as the BCS title game. At most, two teams would play seventeen games, which is one more than some high school state champions.

Bowls would go nowhere—and certainly not out of business, as the Cartel wants you to believe. Their proper place in the college football world—as purveyors of exhibition games in reward for successful seasons and not as ATMs for bowl directors—would return. The bowl system serves a purpose when it serves the sport, and only in that vein should it remain a part of college football. Bowls' desperate plea to uphold history and tradition rings hollow, considering they're nothing more than private businesses with no official ties to universities and suck tens of millions of dollars in profit away from those schools. With on-campus games, the money stays within college athletics.

And the money. Oh, the money. The playoff plan is a legal bank heist, designed to endow the schools rather than burgle them. It would make the advertised BCS payouts of $18 million for the bowls and $21.2 million for the championship look like a pittance. Even the Cartel admits that.

"I am absolutely sure that an NFL-style football playoff would provide maybe three or four times as many dollars . . . than the present system does," Delany said in front of Congress in 2005.

The current bowl system pays college football about $275 million in gross revenue per year. Schools are on the hook for most expenses, including travel, hotel, meals, and unsold tickets from their hefty allotments. For the 2010–11 bowl season, those costs were about $95 million, according to an analysis of fifty-six publicly available NCAA bowl expense documents. This doesn't include coach and administrator bonuses, pre-bowl practice costs, and other expenses. In the end, college football walks away with a collective profit of about $180 million annually.

Delany's projection of a potential $1.1 billion gross is higher than our experts' estimate: $750 million a year for the playoff alone, an especially conservative mark considering the television contracts lavished on conferences in 2010 and 2011. Each of the fifteen games would pay out $25 million per team. Yes, a first-round playoff game would net conferences 18 percent more than the current BCS championship game.

The bowl system would suffer financially. Even after serious cuts to television revenue, our panel concluded, it still could pay out 50 percent of its current rate, or $137.5 million. This plus the playoff revenue totals to 887.5 million postseason dollars waiting to be tapped, an unheard-of sum in amateur athletics. It's the kind of money that makes tradition-crippling conference realignment unnecessary.

As the Cartel yammers on about its system being not just the right way but the only way, this playoff plan shows otherwise—and it's just the beginning.

It's not like we're playoff-design geniuses. What preceded was essentially the model the NCAA uses to run football championships in Division I-AA, Division II, and Division III. (The official term for Division I-AA these days is Football Championship Subdivision, while Division I-A is called Football Bowl Subdivision. We refuse, out of principle, to bother with such silly names.) While the NCAA has its flaws, there is no denying its skill at running national tournaments. It does so with great success and excitement in eighty-eight different sports and divisions in everything from men's basketball to riflery. Everything but Division I-A football.

The association's central office has no power or jurisdiction over major college football's postseason. Officially, the NCAA treats the glass football held by the winning coach after the BCS championship game like it does the stemware on its table: just another piece of crystal.

Delany, Slive, and the others participate in high-level committees that make NCAA policy on all things except the college football postseason, then step outside their NCAA roles, don their BCS hats, and run that, too. Confused? Everyone is. Former NCAA president Cedric Dempsey used to shake his head at the annual deluge of angry mail he'd receive about the BCS, something over which he wielded no power. This is exactly how the Cartel wants it. Let them blame the wrong guy, and let them propose so many different playoff scenarios that the issue gets muddled.

"Advocates of a hypothetical playoff can't agree on how to resolve key playoff questions: who, what, where, and when," BCS executive director Bill Hancock said.

Since we've answered each of those, we might as well ask another question: How?

The first step is exposing the fraudulence that defines the Cartel to its very last fiber.

2 What Could Have Been

Vince Dooley felt a sense of conviction and hope. It was May 1994, and he had arrived at the Southeastern Conference meetings at the Hilton Sandestin Beach Golf Resort & Spa with a solution to college football's postseason problem. Awaiting him in a conference room was a group of fellow power brokers that had a choice: help thrust college football into the future, or maintain the broken status quo.

Dooley greeted them and set up a slide presentation. During his twenty-five seasons as football coach at the University of Georgia, he had established himself as one of the sport's most respected figures. He amassed more influence after taking over as Georgia's athletic director. Dooley knew both the game of college football and the business of college football. He wasn't a crusader as much as a pragmatist, and he hoped the compelling case on those slides would appeal to his fellow SEC athletic directors at their annual get-together in Destin, Florida.

Seven months earlier, the NCAA had formed a high-level committee to study a playoff. Chaired by UCLA chancellor Charles Young, the group looked at every possible facet of a playoff: academic concerns, weather patterns, television schedules. It emerged with a several-hundred-page-long report that it presented to a twenty-five-member panel of football and business royalty that included Dooley. Ideas ranged from a single-game national championship to a sixteen-team playoff. The playoff options would generate a huge influx of cash, which was critical for the majority of schools that depended on football revenue to fund their athletic departments. For the playoff to become a reality, it needed the approval of key stakeholders.

Dooley was an ideal agent for change, and armed with slides that sketched a workable playoff plan, he hoped to bring the SEC on board. He outlined that day a proposal that would preserve the bowl system and create three additional games—two semifinal matchups and a national championship. The plan called for the four teams to be selected after the January 1 bowl games.

As much sense as it made then and still does nearly two decades later, the playoff plan never had a chance. And Dooley realized as much shortly after his presentation ended. He may have won 201 games and a national championship, may have coached Herschel Walker, and may have become a football icon throughout the South, but Dooley was no match for the man who truly ruled the room: Roy Kramer, the commissioner of the SEC.

"I think we'll have another option," Dooley recalled Kramer saying cryptically.

While Dooley had been working with the NCAA's committee, Kramer had helped orchestrate secret negotiations with commissioners of the five other conferences that eventually formed the core of the Cartel and the BCS. To say that the NCAA's appeal to fair play faced a tough crowd when Dooley presented the playoff plan in that Hilton conference room is an understatement.

The conference commissioners had filled the leadership void in college football, and Kramer was the alpha dog. SEC football under Kramer was as cutthroat as the sport has ever been. During his run as commissioner from 1990 to 2002, he pioneered such groundbreaking and profitable ideas as expanding the league to twelve teams and creating the conference championship game.

He piloted the conference during an era of rampant rule-breaking that kept the NCAA infractions committee busy, with all twelve SEC athletic departments racking up at least one major violation conviction during his tenure.

The ACC, Big Ten, Big 12, Big East, Pac-10, and SEC—the six so-called equity conferences that comprised the ruling class of college athletics—didn't object to the concept of a four-team playoff as much as they hated the idea of ceding control to the NCAA. The bowl system allowed equity conferences to hoard more than 85 percent of the postseason revenue. The NCAA-run men's basketball tournament resulted in a slightly more equitable distribution of postseason revenue based on performance, and to a group guided by avarice, such a thing was unacceptable. If the league commissioners were in charge, they could control access to the bowls.

No one debated that a four-team playoff would generate tens of millions of dollars in additional money or that the revenue shares initially would remain similar. It stood to reason that the only participants in the four-team playoff would come from big conferences, because it's not like Sun Belt Conference teams were cracking the top 20, let alone the top 4. But fear of the unknown and unforeseen, of an uprising among the smaller schools, prompted the equity conferences to follow the lead of so many in positions of power: Use strength to squash the minority.

"I don't want to say that Roy and the commissioners were thinking only of the equity part of it," Dooley said. "But it was certainly, obviously, a motivating factor."

Less than two weeks after Dooley's doomed presentation in Florida, Kramer and his cohorts unveiled the precursor of the BCS. The Bowl Alliance, they called it, and the system relied on the same old polls and the same old bowls as part of an attempt to match the Nos. 1 and 2 teams. The NCAA promptly tabled the idea of a four-team playoff. It amounted to surrender.

The Bowl Alliance started in 1995 without the Big Ten and Pac-10, whose refusal to join was, of course, a self-serving reflex. The conferences were determined to protect their lucrative arrangement with the Rose Bowl. Yet in 1998, after they saw an opportunity to make more money through capitulation, the Big Ten and Pac-10 dumped their exclusive agreement with the Rose Bowl. Turns out tradition did have a price. Thus was born the Bowl Championship Series. And to the chagrin of the fans, coaches, and players who seek progress, the Cartel was entrenched.

More than a decade later it remains so, as does its flawed postseason. In the face of compelling evidence against its utility, the BCS engages in revisionist history trying to defend itself. The argument goes that while the BCS may not be perfect, it was the most perfect option at the time. It wasn't, of course, or Dooley would not have clicked from slide to slide in Destin. At that crucial moment in 1994, the Cartel actively chose a flawed BCS over a playoff.

Inaccurate history, confused facts, and unnecessary hyperbole are the bread and butter of the Cartel. To this day, it argues that a playoff is too confusing to run and falsely claims that no one has put forth a legitimate playoff plan.

"Playoff advocates have had an easy ride where they have never been called on to explain exactly how they would create an alternative," Ari Fleischer, the former press secretary for President George W. Bush, told Politico.com when he was hired by the Cartel as a public relations consultant in 2009.

Never any alternatives? Well, there was the NCAA's exhaustive report and Dooley's presentation in 1994. And a $3 billion offer in 1999 from a Swiss group to stage a sixteen-team playoff. CBS itself once presented to the NCAA a three-round playoff that incorporated the then–New Year's Day bowls. Plus there was the joint SEC-ACC plus-one proposal in 2008 outlining an extra championship game after bowl season. And the lengthy eight-team playoff plan the Mountain West Conference authored in 2009. Don't forget the myriad detailed systems drawn up through the years by athletic directors, private businessmen, and even the president of the University of Georgia, Michael Adams, who said, "The current system has lost public confidence and simply does not work."

Fleischer managed to have it backward when he claimed playoff proponents have had a free ride. It's the BCS that has sailed along by not having to defend against a specific plan that all fans understand. The disorganization of the playoff crowd created the sort of gridlock in which the BCS specializes.

3 Obstruction of Justice

Every cartel needs protection, and so May 1, 2009, on Capitol Hill, the BCS unleashed its version. It wasn't a crooked cop or a corrupt government, like the world's other cartels employ. It wasn't even a smooth-talking, Brioni-suit-wearing lawyer with a six-figure retainer. This Cartel trotted out a bowl executive who, within minutes of introducing himself to Congress, may have committed perjury.

Derrick Fox, the CEO of the Alamo Bowl, was the choice to stand next to ACC commissioner John Swofford in front of a House Energy and Commerce subcommittee. Fox's job was to swear to tell the truth, the whole truth, and nothing but the truth—and convince the nation that a college football playoff is a very bad idea.

A playoff would restrain the bowl system and, by extension, its executives, so Fox wanted to persuade Congress that deviating from the BCS carried an inherent and irreparable risk. It was a classic scare tactic, and he employed artifice because the truth was too damaging. Bowl-game costs siphon nearly 40 percent of college football's postseason revenue, money that could replace tax dollars in balancing public schools' athletic-department budgets. The desire of bowl executives to maintain huge salaries and cushy jobs stands in the way of a playoff worth hundreds of millions of additional dollars to the universities. And even though a playoff would cut into revenue, bowls would still survive—just not with the excess riches and prestige to which bowl executives are accustomed.

With such bleakness staring at him, Fox pulled the oratory version of a fumblerooski. He didn't declare that bowl games are mere football contests. No, in the world of the Cartel, they are altruistic endeavors that just happen to involve a bunch of kids playing football.

"Almost all the postseason bowl games are put on by charitable groups, and since up to one-quarter of the proceeds from the games are dedicated to the community, local charities received tens of millions of dollars a year," Fox said.

His thirty-eight words contained three outrageous exaggerations, which, even for Washington, may be a record. Rep. Joe Barton (R-Texas), who chaired the hearings, would later say the comments possibly qualified as "perjury" and "contempt of Congress."

Fox's claims sounded good. No one is against charity. Kill a bowl game, run by some bare-bones, benevolent group, and a poor, homeless child might starve outside a soup kitchen the next winter. It was a line of reasoning that would cause a politician to pause and the public, which would read the unchecked comments in news accounts, to see the pro-bowl argument in a new light.

Tax documents, interviews with bowl directors, and other public records show a much different reality.

Take exaggeration No. 1: "Almost all the postseason bowl games are put on by charitable groups . . ."

Actually, not a single bowl game is run by a group that could be described as a charity under any commonsense definition. The bowls are controlled, in fact, by executive directors who make fabulous coin, treat their business cronies to lavish swag, and celebrate their altogether awesome lives with first-class flights, multiple country-club memberships, and his and her luxury car allowances. Just like Mother Teresa.

Eleven of the thirty-five bowl games scheduled for 2011–12 are privately owned, seven of them by ESPN and another by a fledgling, bootstrap outfit known as the New York Yankees. So nearly a third of bowl games are the opposite of charities. They exist purely and expressly for profit. They even pay taxes.

Reached after his testimony, Fox would not budge. He claimed a multinational corporation such as ESPN, whose parent, The Walt Disney Company, did $38 billion in revenue in 2010, does indeed qualify as a charitable group.

"Well," Fox said, "[Walt Disney is] certainly involved in charitable activities."

It doesn't end there. The remaining twenty-four bowls aren't run by charities, either. They simply enjoy 501(c)(3) nonprofit status from the Internal Revenue Service, which allows them to avoid paying federal, state, and local taxes. It's a sweetheart deal.

Nonprofit is a misnomer of sorts. It doesn't mean there is zero profit involved. It's merely an accounting term for an organization that is mainly devoted to a public purpose and does not distribute its surplus—often vast—to owners or shareholders. Since no specific person or company owns these bowl games, no one can sell them or walk away with tens of millions of dollars. In the meantime, however, those in charge can drain every last penny of revenue out of the nonprofit. Unspent revenue goes into reserves, where it can be tapped later. Nonprofits can spend lavishly on employees, facilities, and programs, the antithesis of the poor, struggling charity the term conjures.

Harvard University, for instance, is the oldest corporation in the United States, founded in 1636 and incorporated in 1650. Yet it enjoys nonprofit status despite having tens of billions in total assets, including an endowment of more than $27 billion. It charges undergraduates $52,650 a year in tuition, fees, and housing. Massachusetts' politicians have attacked Harvard for not having to pay taxes on its considerable investments.

It's no different for bowl games. Major bowl games have major investment portfolios ($25.2 million for the Sugar Bowl), which most years can easily produce millions in returns. Not having to pay taxes on that investment income (hundreds of thousands and even millions of dollars), in addition to annual revenue that can run into the tens of millions, allows bowl directors to cover high salaries, unnecessary costs, and general mismanagement.

In the case of bowl games, nonprofit status isn't something that should elicit sympathy. It's a benefit that helps ensure their affluent existence.

As for Fox's "charity" line, while nearly all charities—say, the American Cancer Society or the Salvation Army—are nonprofits, not all nonprofits are charities. To imply so, as Fox did under oath in front of Congress, smacked of manipulative doublespeak and opportunism.

"You've got to remember, when you're looking at nonprofit [bowl games] there really is a difference [from] a United Way," said Jim McVay, CEO of the Outback Bowl, when told of Fox's statement. "There's a difference in economics."

In other words, calling bowls "almost all" charities might score emotional points with meddling lawmakers and media, but it just isn't the truth.

Fox was just getting started. Exaggeration No. 2—"up to one-quarter of the proceeds from the games are dedicated to the community . . ."—was a whopper.

Before we get to what bowl games give—and it's frighteningly little—let's start with what they take. The twenty-three games with records publicly available at the time of Fox's testimony received $7.5 million in direct government handouts, according to their federal tax filings. That's straight cash. It doesn't factor in the estimated millions from police and fire department detail work, traffic control, cleanup, and other public services donated to the games by local governments that assume the overtime costs.

The Sugar Bowl, for instance, received $3 million in direct funding from the Louisiana state government, according to its fiscal 2007 tax filing, the applicable return for Fox's comments. The government assistance is so important to the Sugar Bowl that the game paid a lobbying firm in Baton Rouge to ensure its public financing.

With the bowl receiving so much, then, it stands to reason that what Fox considers a charitable group would reciprocate the giving. The Sugar Bowl brought in $34.1 million in revenue that year, according to its tax form. One quarter of that, per Fox's testimony, would be about $8.525 million.

The Sugar Bowl says it gave $100,000 in fiscal 2007 to help rebuild a local park damaged by Hurricane Katrina. That's 0.29 percent of revenue—less than one-third of 1 percent. In a purely semantic way, Fox was right, because the Sugar Bowl did contribute "up to one-quarter" to charity. It just fell a tiny bit short— about $8.425 million.

Fox's confusion over what was and wasn't given is somewhat understandable. Bowl-game generosity isn't easy to track. In the original edition of this book, we reported that the Sugar Bowl gave zero dollars to charity in fiscal 2007 because it failed to list any donations on its federal tax form. Josh Peter, one of the authors of this book, then interviewed Sugar Bowl CEO Paul Hoolahan three times, including discussions on charitable giving overall and the accuracy of Fox's comments in general.

In conversations both on and off the record, Hoolahan never mentioned the $100,000. He said the game's fiscal 2007 tax return was correct, perhaps also unaware that there was no donation listed. Hoolahan's spokesman later said, "He has no recollection of any conversation regarding the charitable contributions of the bowl."

After the first edition of this book was published, the bowl noted that it had given the $100,000 gift that year, part of a multiyear commitment. We asked the bowl to provide records of the donation, which it agreed to do. That was in November 2010. As of press time in summer 2011, we still hadn't received the documentation.

Not that it matters. We checked out the park and it looks great. So we're happy to take the Sugar Bowl's word for it and let the facts continue to speak volumes: In fiscal 2007, the Sugar Bowl effectively gave back $100,000 of the $3 million it took from the Louisiana state government, which the following year ran a $341 million deficit.

It's not like the Sugar Bowl lacked money to give. Nor did it even need the government subsidy, because the $3 million they lobbied out of government coffers only padded the profit margin. The $34.1 million in revenue was offset by just $22.5 million in expenses, so it turned an $11.6 million, tax-free profit. The bowl ended that fiscal year with $37 million in assets—which was necessary, since the Sugar Bowl's checkbook is a sieve otherwise.

In 2008, Hoolahan received $609,225 in salary and other compensation, according to Sugar Bowl tax records. The next year, his total package jumped to $645,386. Hoolahan's assistant executive director, Jeff Hundley, took in $375,732 and $398,023, respectively, in those same years.

Don't forget the lifestyle that comes with outrageous expense accounts, travel budgets, and a bank account padded annually by the state. The following expenditures are real. They come from the Sugar Bowl's tax returns from 2005, 2006, and 2007:

- $494,177 on "entertainment" (2005)
- $188,305 on "Hall of Fame" (2005)
- $201,226 on "gifts and bonuses" (2007)
- $684,578 on "media relations" (2007)
- $330,244 on "decorations" (2007)
- $114,666 on "committee meetings" (2006)
- $46,017 on "conference meetings" (2006)
- $91,983 on "conference relations" (2007)
- $58,995 on "liaison" (2006)
- $158,030 on "Allstate [Insurance] liaison" (2007)
- $447,817 on "Sugar Bowl event-related entertainment" (2007)
- $810,833 on "BCS Championship event-related entertainment" (2007)
- $82,884 on "other expenses" (2006)
- $260,062 on "other expenses" (2007)

On and on it goes. The Sugar Bowl has an actual "committee on golf" and a "special subcommittee on ladies' entertainment"—which may or may not have anything to do with all those "liaisons."

The Sugar Bowl is no different than its brethren. The Orange Bowl spent $42,281 on golf in fiscal years 2004 and 2006 and annually drops six figures on "postage and shipping." The Sugar and Orange sometimes pay first-class airfare for not just their CEOs but spouses as well. It helps explain how the Orange Bowl could rack up $756,546 in travel costs in fiscal 2009. The Fiesta picked up part of the tax bill for some executives, a practice known as gross-up payments, and doled out interest-free loans.

Numerous bowls, BCS or otherwise, provided complimentary cars for directors and their wives.

Bowls have no qualms with plying ADs and conference commissioners with golf weekends, booze, dinners, gifts, mani-pedis for spouses, and whatever else it takes them to remain college football's postseason. Bowl executives long ago understood that top recruits aren't the only thing for sale in college football.

Although there is a complaint pending to the IRS about excessive executive pay, undisclosed lobbying, and other irregularities, some of the expenditures appear completely legal. In most cases, the Sugar Bowl can spend its money any way it wants. It can decorate the whole French Quarter if it so chooses. Look at the Music City Bowl. In 2003, officials at the Nashville bowl spent $7,203 on an office miniature golf tournament, according to *The Orange County Register*. Surely Tennesseans are thrilled to know that the bowl that put on a nearly five-figure putt-putt match received upward of a half-million dollars in public funding since 2006.

Back to Fox and his third exaggeration: "local charities received tens of millions of dollars a year."

One look at the available records at the time of Fox's testimony in 2009, plus follow-up interviews with representatives of nearly every bowl, showed Fox wildly embellished the truth of the games' generosity.

The approximate total payout to charities: a combined $3.3 million.

The bowls could give tens of millions of dollars a year; the tax-exempt bowls produced $186 million in revenue that year. And they combined to give just 1.7 percent of it to charity. Even worse, those bowls ended their fiscal years with $141 million in net assets, including more than $80 million in cash reserves.

"That doesn't seem like something that's really geared toward giving to charity, does it?" Rep. Barton said.

It seems like a calculated exaggeration meant to confuse Congress and the public. Barton didn't realize Fox's misrepresentation until informed by us soon after the testimony and long after the media disseminated the comments as fact.

Even fellow bowl executives couldn't defend Fox's claims. They know they aren't "charitable groups," no matter what Fox said under oath. They are under no obligation to give any money to charity, which is why some don't. More than half of the $3.3 million in charitable contributions came from just two bowl games, the Orange and the Chick-fil-A.

Others spread meager, largely symbolic donations around the area. The Florida Citrus Sports Association, which runs two Orlando-based games, donated just $10,570 of its $12.4 million in revenue to charities, according to its fiscal 2008 tax returns. One lucky recipient: the Pace Center for Girls, which received $120.

Others followed loose interpretations of *community* and *local*. The Fiesta Bowl used its fortune to aid organizations that "appear to be aligned with [CEO John] Junker's political views," according to an internal report. That included thousands to the Acton Institute, which strives to integrate "Judeo-Christian truths with free-market principles," and the Bio-Ethics Defense Fund, a pro-life law firm and lobbying group operated by what the bowl acknowledged was one of Junker's friends.

"If Derrick [Fox] made that comment, that kind of invites, 'OK, let's go see how many tens of millions were involved here,'" said Hoolahan, the Sugar Bowl executive. "That sounds a little hyperbolic in the heat of battle."

Well, it came from a statement prepared in advance of the hearings. And Fox didn't back down in a phone interview, claiming his comments were fair and accurate, the information having been provided by the Football Bowl Association. In that conversation, Fox did concede it would be ridiculous to include as charitable donations the payouts bowl games make to participating teams. He later flip-flopped on that subject, telling media in San Antonio that bowl payouts should count as charitable contributions. By that logic, in Fox's world, Nick Saban and Mack Brown count as "local charities."

"To use the words 'local charities,' I assume it goes to the Boys & Girls Club, the YMCA," Barton said.

For his part, John Swofford offered cover for the Cartel, using his stature as the ACC commissioner to support and praise Fox. (Swofford later declined our request to discuss his testimony.) If Swofford had an even cursory knowledge of bowl finances—and you'd suspect he does—he complied with Fox's exaggeration in triplicate.

"None of us in college football are anxious to jeopardize . . . the many . . . charitable endeavors undertaken by all of the bowl games," Swofford testified. He later added, "the bowls and the host cities have been very good to the game. . . . They have been loyal supporters . . . and merit our full support."

The lawmakers weren't completely duped. Barton kept blasting away with critical questions and claimed that the BCS is "like communism. You can't fix it." Though he couldn't lie: The charitable stuff had sounded good at the time. No politician wanted to filch money from a local cause.

Like much of the BCS, however, what gets said, even under oath, doesn't match up with reality.

4 Lies, Damn Lies, and Bowl Payouts

It was December 2008, three weeks from kickoff, and the Motor City Bowl still needed a team to play Central Michigan. When the regular season ended, seventy-one teams had been bowl-eligible by virtue of winning at least six games. Bids went out. Matchups were set. Now only five teams remained available to the Motor City Bowl and its executive director, Ken Hoffman.

Rather than court any of those teams, he waited for his phone to ring.

A flurry of calls ensued, and Hoffman checked the incoming numbers. Area code 408. It was athletic officials from San Jose State. Area code 561. Florida Atlantic wanted in. Thus commenced a bidding war, though not the traditional sort. The schools were bargaining for the right to play in the Motor City Bowl, and the winner would be whichever decided to take the least money out of the game's advertised $750,000-per-team payout.

San Jose State offered to take just $250,000 and accept the rest in face-value tickets, even though those tickets would be hard to give away, much less sell, for an anonymous bowl game in iced-over Detroit.

Florida Atlantic offered to relinquish all cash and, as compensation, take $750,000 in tickets to a stadium that would have tens of thousands of empty seats. For the honor of playing in a no-name bowl, Florida Atlantic was willing to be paid nothing. Soon, Hoffman announced the Motor City Bowl's matchup. Central Michigan's opponent would be Florida Atlantic. And the media continued to report a payout of $750,000 per team.

To paraphrase Mark Twain, there are three kinds of lies: lies, damned lies, and bowl payouts.

Bowl games advertise big, flashy checks going to the teams, which leaves fans with the impression that they're profitable and beneficial for every participating team and part of a positive system that must, at all costs, be preserved.

Sorry, but it's all a shell game, a backward system affecting the Granddaddy of Them All down to the Lowliest of Them All. When athletic departments compare actual payouts with expenses, the collective profits are dramatically slimmer than advertised, and the bowl system is more shakedown than moneymaker. The majority of bowl games leave schools in the red, requiring conferences to pool bowl payouts and take revenue generated by BCS games to cover the losses from lower-tier ones, such as the Motor City Bowl.

Bowl games don't pay for transportation. Or lodging. Or most of the teams' meals. So shortly after cutting the deal with the Motor City Bowl, Florida Atlantic athletic director Craig Angelos sat in his office trying to figure out how avoid losing hundreds of thousands of dollars. He's the rare AD who doesn't get a bonus just for reaching a money-losing bowl game. He's rewarded for balancing the department budget, and he needed to figure out how to do that for a game that paid Florida Atlantic nothing.

He decided to leave behind the school's marching band and instead partner with a high school band in Detroit, resulting in a savings of $80,000. And he arranged for the team to fly home right after the game rather than spend another night in a hotel, which would've cost $10,000. And to bring in only six cheer-leaders and a mascot one day before the game, which set him back only $1,090. Even with the scrimping and scratching, and with more than a quarter million dollars given to the program by the Sun Belt Conference, Florida Atlantic still needed to come up with $41,196 to cover its 126-person traveling party for the Motor City Bowl, money the nonexistent payout never reimbursed.

"The good news is you get to go to a bowl game," Angelos said. "The heavy lifting comes when you're trying to make the numbers work."

Often the numbers don't work and end up costing schools hundreds of thousands and even millions of dollars, an exami-nation of public records shows. Going to a bowl game is no cheap affair. Travel costs can be exorbitant. Ohio State spent $2 million on transportation, rooms, meals, and entertainment for its appearance in the 2010 Rose Bowl.

Part of the problem is bowls often contractually obligate schools to stay for a certain number of nights (up to eight), usu-ally at top-of-the-line hotels—$250 a night and up. Sometimes schools are forced to rent more rooms—up to 500—than they have live bodies, leaving them paying for empty beds.

Bowls demand such absurdities because of kickbacks from local hotels. The Sugar Bowl listed $191,587 in revenue from "Hotel/Motel Commission" on its 2009 federal tax form. The payout comes from the Greater New Orleans Hotel and Lodging Association and, according to bowl spokesman John Sudsbury, is "a voluntary program where hotels provide the Bowl with a commission on room nights used in conjunction with the Sugar Bowl and/or BCS Championship Game." While the bowl doesn't know which hotels donate, they essentially pass a six-figure tax on to the universities. The Fiesta Bowl has a similar twenty-year arrangement with Scottsdale hotels. The Orange Bowl declined to discuss the issue.

Then there are the soaring bonuses tied to bowl-game appearances for coaches and athletic department staffers. Alabama paid nearly $1.3 million in bonuses after the 2010 BCS championship game. Combine that with travel requirements, and Alabama spent a total of $4.3 million on the game, $1.8 million more than allocated by the SEC.

Yes, even the national champion can lose nearly $2 million winning its title. For the 2011 title game, the winner (Auburn) and loser (Oregon) lost $614,106 and $312,437, respectively.

Beyond the championship game, the most onerous part of the bowl racket is the so-called ticket guarantee, which requires teams to buy thousands of full-price seats they can rarely resell in full. Since so few games sell out, fans know to wait for prices to plummet online. On the day of the 2009 Music City Bowl, tickets were available for 19 cents on StubHub. Kentucky and Clemson officials may have been foolish enough to pay full price (up to $70) for 10,500 tickets, as the bowl contract required, but their fans weren't.

Seventy teams participated in the thirty-five bowl games during the 2010–11 season. Fourteen are not subject to open-records laws. We received bowl expense data from the other fifty-six. Using that and estimations built on similar games, travel distance, and ticket guarantees, we extrapolated the total cost for college football. Including travel, lodging, entertainment, and other costs, schools spent an estimated $95 million attending bowl games, and that doesn't include bonuses, which some schools failed to provide on their expense forms. That's a near-nine-figure subsidy for the bowl industry.

Ticket guarantees hit schools with an estimated $24.1 million alone. The ugliest number of all: Universities that played in bowl games spent $20.1 million more than their conference allotted them, a veritable Red Sea.

This is the illusion of bowl payouts: big dollars trumpeted loudly, costs rarely acknowledged.

It's been that way for years. In 2008, the Papajohns.com Bowl advertised a payout of $300,000 per team yet required both schools to buy 10,000 tickets, which cost each athletic department $400,000. While Rutgers beat North Carolina State 29–23, nearly half of the 71,594-seat Legion Field in Birmingham, Alabama, sat empty. Television producers had fans sit on one side of the stadium so it looked crowded. Nothing could hide that both teams were financial losers. For $300,000 and a pizza bowl appearance, N.C. State spent $730,000 and Rutgers spent almost $1.2 million.

In Rutgers' case, the school sold just 4,650 tickets, absorbing a loss of $214,000 off the bat. Qualifying for a bowl game triggered bonuses for the coaches, almost $270,000 worth of extra pay for leading the school to a game that resulted in hundreds of thousands of dollars in losses. Not that Rutgers coach Greg Schiano can be blamed for the out-of-control expenses that make these games so popular among Cartel members. Rutgers epitomized wasteful spending.

Twenty-one Rutgers executives and administrators spent $28,950 getting to and from the game ($1,378.57 per person). On the ground, they blew an additional $60,168 over six days. That's an average of $478 a day on room, food, and booze—no small feat in Birmingham, Alabama.

At the time, Rutgers was coming off a New Jersey state audit into the school's spending for its trip to the 2006 Texas Bowl. The investigation found that the school had violated its own expense policies. Spending was out of control, with $11,000 going to such incidentals as in-room movies and valet parking.

The University of Iowa spent $328,340 for its band to attend the 2009 Outback Bowl. It wasn't only for transportation, hotels, and meals, either. The Outback doesn't miss a beat when bilking a participating university.

The Hawkeye Marching Band provided free halftime entertainment for the game, allowing Tampa Bay Bowl Association Inc. to avoid hiring a professional act, which cost the Orange Bowl $531,250 in 2009, according to tax records. Rather than show its appreciation for a free performance, the Outback charged Iowa $65 per game ticket for each of the 346 members of the band's traveling party. Total cost: $22,490. In bowl games, not even the band gets in free.

It's not like the Outback was hurting for the money, either. It turned a profit on that game and ended fiscal 2010 with $9.5 million in assets, according to tax records—no surprise, considering bowls have figured out how to make money on halftime.

The Outback Bowl isn't the lone guilty party. Poor Iowa got hit even worse in 2010, when the school spent $457,307 to bring its marching-band members to the Orange Bowl—including $51,000 on tickets just to get them into the game, according to university records. The only people not charged for tickets at most bowl games are the players and coaches. And these are the entities that the bowl system is so happy to paint as "partners" with the schools. What the Cartel calls a partnership is actually a fleecing.

Even the biggest programs at the biggest games suffer. Ohio State was obligated to buy 17,500 tickets to the 2009 Fiesta Bowl, according to NCAA records. It sold 9,983, losing a cool $1 million. Florida ate $1 million on the 2010 Sugar Bowl ticket guarantee, part of a $212,125 loss the school took on the BCS game with an advertised payout of $17.5 million.

Virginia Tech sold less than 20 percent of its required 17,500-ticket allotment for the 2009 Orange Bowl, according to school documents. The Hokies and the ACC combined to pay full price for 14,158 empty seats to the game. Net loss: $1.77 million. It was part of an epic bath that the Orange Bowl laid on the school. Virginia Tech's expense allowance from the ACC was $1.6 million. It spent $3.8 million. Even UConn, whose first BCS bowl appearance in the 2011 Fiesta morphed into a fiscal disaster in which it swallowed $2.9 million in tickets, lost less than Virginia Tech's $2.2 million.

"So many of those bowls are costly to universities," Boise State president Bob Kustra said. "When the BCS bowl ends up costing Connecticut, you know something is broken. It's become almost an entitlement, which I think is dead wrong. Coaches and athletic directors think there must be a bowl in postseason play even if we didn't do that well during the season. If there's any reform, even before BCS reform, we ought to figure out how to restructure that.

"Everybody's lobbying for a bigger, stronger bowl. Right here, in Boise, the Humanitarian Bowl is a perfect example. It's not easy for me to say, but it doesn't make sense as a football event."

West Virginia had $507,000 in tickets to the 2010 Champs Sports Bowl go unsold. Michigan and the Big Ten were forced to absorb $510,145 in seats to the 2011 Gator Bowl. Clemson and South Florida combined to spend $1,053,840 on tickets to the 2010 Meineke Car Care Bowl, just edging out the $1,007,615 the Liberty Bowl ticket deal gave Georgia and Central Florida. Texas Tech dropped $473,475 all alone on seats to the TicketCity Bowl, even though it was in Dallas, near so many Red Raider alums. Throw in over half a million in travel costs and Tech went $651,477 over allotment. Western Michigan was required to pay $450,000 for eleven thousand tickets to its 2008 Texas Bowl game against Rice, according to the *San Diego Union-Tribune*. The Broncos sold just 548, leaving them $412,535 in the hole.

Summary of Postseason Football Institutional Bowl Expenses for 2008–09

Participating institution: Virginia Polytechnic Institute & State University
Name of bowl game: Orange Bowl
Date of bowl game: January 1, 2009

PARTICIPATING INSTITUTION'S REVENUE

Expense allowance from conference (if applicable):	$ 1,600,000

PARTICIPATING INSTITUTION'S EXPENSES

Transportation costs (please list):

Team and staff total cost:	$ 183,524
Number of days traveled:	8
Number in travel party:	171
Band and cheerleaders total cost:	**$ 101,607**
Number of days traveled:	7
Number in travel party:	434
Official party (faculty, athletics dept., etc.) total cost:	**$ 102,964**
Number of days traveled:	8
Number in travel party:	136
Subtotal Transportation Expense:	**$ 388,095**

Meals/Lodging Per Diem:

Team and staff:	$ 446,283
Band and cheerleaders:	$ 258,329
Official party (faculty, athletics dept., etc.):	$ 66,776
SUBTOTAL MEALS/LODGING PER DIEM EXPENSE:	**$ 771,388**

Entertainment:	$ 40,000
Promotion:	$ 11,541
Awards:	$ 80,995
Equipment and supplies:	$ 69,800
*Tickets (line 3.c. from below):	$ 1,769,750
Administrative:	$ 100,907
Other (please detail below):	$ 586,428
supplemental compensation, wages, FICA	
TOTAL EXPENSES:	**$ 3,818,904**

Should include only the amount the institution and/or conference absorbed from unsold tickets.

PARTICIPATING INSTITUTION'S TICKET COMMITMENT

	Number	Ticket Price	Total
1) Tickets committed:			
a. By institution	6,750	$ 125	$ 843,750
b. By conference	10,750	$ 125	$ 1,343,750
2) Tickets sold:			
a. By institution	3,342	$ 125	$ 417,750
b. By conference	0	$ 125	$ 0
3) Tickets absorbed:			
a. By institution	3,408	$ 125	$ 426,000
b. By conference	10,750	$ 125	$ 1,343,750
c. Total of tickets absorbed:	**14,158**	**$ 125**	**$ 1,769,750**

"Half to two-thirds of all bowl ticket sales are basically a money push," Mountain West commissioner Craig Thompson said. "I've got to pay for my ten thousand tickets, so here's my check for $600,000. Then you pay me the $750,000 'bowl payout.' Why even go through the charade? Why don't I just buy the 3,800 tickets my fans want? Or don't make me buy tickets and don't pay me anything.

"They only do it for the public relations value. It isn't a real figure. They've just inflated it and come up with this $750,000 number because it sounds good."

Sounding good matters most to bowl games. Six bowls—the Capital One, Cotton, Independence, Las Vegas, Motor City, and Famous Idaho Potato—actually pay less in inflation-adjusted money today than they did in 1998. And that's just if you believe their listed payouts, which the Motor City proves aren't real.

Creative accounting helps preserve the illusion that all bowl games are profitable for schools. Most conferences pool bowl payouts, allowing a BCS bid to cover the costs for money-losing mid- and lower-tier bowls. According to official BCS payout documents, the power conferences were guaranteed at least $19.8 million in 2010. Many conferences cut each school a check even if it didn't participate in the postseason. Others offer extra for participating teams to defray costs.

Whether the school or conference eats unsold tickets—the popular spin declares that the conference assumes all unsold tickets, allowing the individual athletic directors an easy out for lost money—since most conferences pool all bowl money, the end result is the same. Unsold tickets result in smaller payouts from conferences. It's robbing Peter to pay Paul. The system allows lower-tier bowl teams to live off the welfare of BCS bowl teams, yet in the grand scheme, the pooling of bowl revenue costs everyone millions.

The University of Florida's appearance in the 2009 BCS title game came with an advertised payout of $17.5 million. That may have sounded good. The SEC allotment for the Gators was just $2.467 million, though.

Among coaches' bonuses ($960,000), travel costs ($788,000), tickets ($288,750), a meeting room at the hotel ($40,000), and other expenses, the total to scoot across the state to Miami Gardens ate up just about everything. For winning the 2009 BCS championship game, Florida cleared $650 in operational expenses, according to university records. Yes, $650.

"There is a perception that we make $17 million because the public sees that payout number, but the data doesn't show that," Florida spokesman Steve McClain told the *Sun-Sentinel*.

The bowl business is particularly lucrative because it dictates financial terms even though schools develop the product, market it, and bring the customers. Colleges take a paddling, come back the next year, and say, "Thank you, sir! May I have another?"

Perhaps nothing illustrates it as well as Virginia Tech, victim of the $2.2 million bleeder in the '09 Orange Bowl. The Hokies opened their 2010–11 season playing Boise State at FedEx Field in Maryland, a game put on by Washington Redskins management, which owns and operates the stadium and was trying to tap new revenue streams by holding college football games. Virginia Tech ended the year playing in the Orange Bowl again.

The first deal was negotiated in the free marketplace. Virginia Tech could've chosen another neutral-site game or just stayed home. That allowed the school to fetch a reasonable—and profitable—contract. The bowl game couldn't have been any more different. The school's only course of action in the face of a lopsided, sure-to-be-million-dollar-loser of a deal was to decline a BCS bowl. To do so would require facing the wrath of fans, media, and rival coaches who would question the Hokies' commitment to the sport. It's essentially no choice at all, something the bowls understand. In recent years, only Notre Dame, an independent private school, has turned down a bowl invitation—and certainly not to a BCS game.

To play Boise State in the opener, Virginia Tech was paid $2.35 million, according to the university contract obtained through an open-records request. The Redskins picked up "reasonable and customary actual travel expenses," including "bus rental and hotel costs." It offered another $5,000 for incidental game-day operation expenses. There were free parking spots and a few gratis luxury boxes.

To play in the Orange Bowl, Tech was given a $1.725 million cut from the ACC. The rest of the advertised payout went mostly to cover bowl losses incurred by other teams in the conference. Virginia Tech was left to pick up virtually all travel costs.

Unlike the trip to suburban Washington, D.C., which allowed the school to choose its accommodations, length of stay, and size of traveling party, the Orange Bowl contract determined everything. Virginia Tech needed to rent 150 rooms for seven nights at the Westin Diplomat Resort and Spa at $212 per night. There were an additional 200 rooms for three nights—cost: $258 per night—at the same hotel. Plus another 125 rooms for three nights at the Sheraton Fort Lauderdale Beach Hotel for $175 a night. And the ACC itself was on the hook for fifteen rooms at the Ritz-Carlton Key Biscayne at $319 per night. The total: 490 rooms for $457,380—before taxes, surcharges, parking, and other incidentals. Not including the ACC's Ritz bill, the school spent $503,298 on hotel stays alone.

The Redskins didn't require the Hokies to sell a block of seats at inflated prices. They actually provided 1,050 complimentary tickets. Those were good for the marching band, players' families, university personnel, and others. Bowl games cackle at the idea. Complimentary tickets? Why would we let the band or the players' parents in for free when we can make the school pay for it? Those 1,050 seats Redskins owner Daniel Snyder gave away would have fetched the Orange Bowl another quarter million.

Virginia Tech had to buy 17,500 tickets to the bowl game at up to $225 per seat. By kickoff, tickets cost less than $20 through online resellers. That was the university's problem, of course. The Orange Bowl was getting $2,276,255 from the school in guaranteed sales. Virginia Tech grinned and gritted its teeth, got hammered 40–12 by Stanford, and came up $1.6 million short in the end. Virginia Tech students and their families, meanwhile, paid $6.5 million in student fees during the 2009–10 academic year so the athletic department could balance its books.

The knee-jerk criticism toward schools for not "traveling well" is often a shift-the-blame ploy created by bowl directors. When allowed to operate in the free market, Virginia Tech cleared close to $2.35 million. The much-derided Snyder proved a far more generous business collaborator than Tech's so-called partner in the bowl game.

Regular-season game promoters say the starting rate for a major program at a neutral site is $2 million, plus expenses. Yet those very teams, when forced into bowl contracts, are lucky to break even and often get crushed. Unrealized gains are the true cost here. Any business that suffers from inefficient operations, duplicate services, and outdated contracts that drive up expenses and eat into earnings doesn't sit idly and shrug its shoulders. It does everything in its power to correct the practices. Lost profits count as lost money. Except in college football.

Certainly there are ancillary benefits to a BCS game. The Orange Bowl's 6.7 television rating exposed Virginia Tech to a vast audience. Then again, so did the Boise State–Tech game, which drew a 7.3 rating. However much extra merchandise money or alumni donations or other revenue streams came from the BCS appearance, they almost assuredly didn't match the $4 million difference between the Boise game and the bowl game. It did raise the question, Why do schools have to pay for the right to play football? Other than the Orange Bowl needing the money to dole out free Caribbean cruises to ACC administrators who, in turn, allow the racket to continue.

Bowl directors estimate that only fourteen of the thirty-five games generate a legitimate profit for the participating teams. While the twenty-one other bowls place additional burden on the schools and conferences, they serve the BCS backers well. When the outcry for a playoff swells, the standard reply includes such tired flimflam as a playoff could jeopardize the future of these bowl games and deny athletes the cherished bowl-game trip experience.

Sanity reared its noble head, however briefly, in 2001, when the Humanitarian Bowl courted a 7-4 UCLA team. The Bruins had started 6-0 and appeared to be a contender for the national championship before they lost three of their last four games. Despite the late-season swoon, they remained an appealing team for a low-tier game like the Humanitarian Bowl, played on the signature blue turf in Boise.

Pete Dalis, then in his last year as UCLA's athletic director, ended the talks before Humanitarian Bowl officials made a formal offer. Then, as now, the Humanitarian Bowl advertised a payout of $750,000 per team—a claim that warrants fine print and full disclosure. Dalis, in explaining his decision, turned into a bowl-game whistleblower. He cited the Humanitarian's requirements—such as the responsibility for selling 5,000 tickets at $33 each, a donation in the form of a "corporate sponsorship," and a minimum stay of five nights in Boise—and said that UCLA stood to lose $300,000 if it accepted a bid to a game that advertised a payout of $750,000.

"UCLA felt a fiduciary responsibility to at least break even in the bowl game," Dalis said at the time. "We never said we weren't interested in playing in the game, just unwilling to lose several hundred thousand dollars to play."

Nine years later, fiduciary responsibility remains little more than a quaint notion. Case in point: In December 2008, losing money was a secondary concern for San Jose State and Florida Atlantic, then both 6-6 after the regular season and chiefly concerned about getting into a bowl game. Their hopes—or perhaps delusions—were that the publicity and visibility associated with a bowl-game appearance would pay off in recruiting, fundraising, and ticket sales. That December, when it cut its deal with the Motor City Bowl, Florida Atlantic felt it needed every possible jolt in hopes of building a new home on its Boca Raton, Florida, campus by the 2010 season.

The school had approved the construction of a 30,000-seat stadium and was still looking for private donations to close the financial gap for the $62 million project. The goal: a fall 2010 opening. Until then, Florida Atlantic would play its home games at Lockhart Stadium, an 18,500-seat stadium fifteen miles from campus and light years from the elite facilities of big-time college football. Florida Atlantic desperately wanted to be big-time, so it scraped the money together, did its belt-tightening as best it could to make its way to Detroit, and walked out onto the field for the Motor City Bowl a proud team.

With their cheerleaders and mascot arriving at the last minute, with their high school band in place, with their travel party thinned like a wrestler trying to shave off those last few ounces, the Florida Atlantic Owls took the field and delivered an upset with a 24–21 victory over Central Michigan. Soon enough, the Owls would begin to evaluate the early returns on their bowl-trip investment.

On national signing day two months after the victory, Florida Atlantic signed twenty-six recruits, and Rivals.com ranked the class eighty-ninth among Division I-A teams. None of the twenty-six players who signed with the Owls lived anywhere near Detroit. All but one hailed from Florida. At least they were eighty-ninth. It was better than Florida Atlantic's classes of 2008 (101st) and 2007 (118th).

It didn't last. On signing day in 2010, Florida Atlantic hauled in the 120th-ranked class in the country, according to Rivals .com. Its batch of recruits was considered the worst of the seven biggest programs in Florida. It was the worst, too, in the nine-team Sun Belt, generally regarded as the weakest conference in major college football. Florida Atlantic's class, in fact, was rated the lowest in all of Division I-A football: 120th of 120 teams.

Those recruits didn't get to see the new stadium until their sophomore year. In August 2009, citing the economic downturn, Florida Atlantic announced the scheduled opening had been delayed by a year. Michigan State canceled its trip to Boca Raton in 2010. The contract specified that the Spartans would meet the Owls in the new stadium. Big Ten teams, and big-time teams, don't do tiny stadiums.

Big-time teams don't lose multiple games in the worst conference in America, either. In 2009, Florida Atlantic finished 5-7 and failed to qualify for a bowl game. A year later, it went 4-8. There was no sign of a return on investment from the Motor City Bowl excursion. And anyone who thinks dividends will be realized in time should take heed of what Dalis told *USA Today* after he paid attention to the bottom line and refused to lose money on a trip to a bowl game.

"I think a lot of schools feel very strongly that, no matter what the cost, they have to go to a bowl game," he said. "In my nineteen years in this business, I've found they really don't alter the future. I think it's a myth."

Mark Twain would have been less polite. He would have called the advertised bowl payouts what they really are.

A lie.

5 A Fiesta for All

All you need to know about the bowl system comes in one handy package. No amount of rhetoric could emasculate the games quite like a single document released March 29, 2011. Over the previous four months, a group of lawyers hired by the Fiesta Bowl's board of directors to investigate alleged corruption rooted through 55 gigabytes of data, ten thousand scanned documents, and thousands of paper records. They conducted eighty-seven interviews. They issued a 276-page report that detailed every bit of misappropriation, from possibly illegal campaign contributions to the very last dollar spent in strip clubs. And in the process, they brought down the man who helped build the Fiesta Bowl into a money-making juggernaut and set a standard of opulence that slithered through the rest of the system.

Pick a page, practically any page, and John Junker's name appears. The report cites him more than five hundred times, almost always in unflattering terms. Like how Junker used Fiesta funds to funnel tens of thousands of dollars to his pet politicians. Or Junker's yearly credit-card ledgers that show $4,856,680 expensed to the bowl over the past decade—an average of $1,330 a day, every single day, for ten years. Nothing crystallizes the bowl system—its incestuous gift-giving, its quid-pro-quo standard, its survival-of-the-richest ethos—quite like one charge on March 24, 2003.

Junker loved golf. The Fiesta Bowl paid $18,926.34 a year for his club memberships. He once charged $2,285.96 worth of Nike golf equipment to the bowl because he was headed to a Nike tournament and didn't want to use gear that might anger one of his game's big sponsors. And when he was trying to curry favor—and John Junker spent all twenty-one of his years running the Fiesta trying to curry favor—he would plop down his AMEX on something like a round of golf with Jack Nicklaus for $95,000, as he did in March 2003.

To complete the foursome, Junker invited Kevin Weiberg (then the Big 12 commissioner), Mark Womack (the SEC associate commissioner), and John Compton (president of Frito-Lay, whose Tostitos are the title sponsor for the Fiesta). Weiberg canceled. Junker filled the final spot with . . . himself. And there he was, the man who always wore the canary-colored blazer, who the report alleges took human growth hormone and charged it to his employer, who threw himself a $33,188.96 birthday party on the company dime, playing eighteen with the Golden Bear. Living, by God, the good life.

It ended eight years later on March 29, 2011. The Fiesta Bowl fired Junker that day. The greatest perpetrator of college football's culture of cronyism ended up its first victim. The Arizona attorney general's office is looking into Junker's reimbursing employees in the form of a "bonus" for their contributions to politicians. The BCS announced it would launch its own investigation into the Fiesta's worthiness as part of its core four bowl games—and, naturally, named to its "task force" Southern Mississippi athletic director Richard Giannini, who less than a year earlier accepted a free Caribbean cruise from the Orange Bowl.

One guy on the take judging another. So goes the BCS circle of life.

In the Fiesta Bowl's 1969 articles of incorporation, the game's forbears laid out certain ideals for the game to follow. One of those is as follows: "[N]o part of its net earning or assets shall ever . . . benefit any private shareholder or individual." Another: "All funds not paid to the participating colleges shall be used by the corporation for educational and charitable purposes."

By the end of John Junker's tenure, the Fiesta was abiding by a set of rules so equal and opposite they were practically Newtonian. Officials at Arizona State started the Fiesta to ensure their football team, then in the WAC, would participate in a bowl of some sort. Less than twenty years later, when the thirty-four-year-old Junker took over the Fiesta and vowed not to let it get "lost in the maze of eight or nine bowl games on New Year's Day," the Fiesta had hosted what passed for the national championship twice. In 1996, the Fiesta partnered with the Sugar and Orange bowls in the Bowl Alliance and joined the rotation for the official championship game. And it supplanted the Cotton Bowl, more than thirty years its elder, because of Junker's brilliance in leveraging his resources toward the right people.

The spilling of the Fiesta Bowl's innermost secrets revealed what long has been suspected of bowl games: They operate in a netherworld of graft and artifice where they steal money from a patsy (the schools), use it to lavish the rainmakers (commissioners, ADs, and politicians), and expect their backs to remain sufficiently scratched. The Fiesta, with Junker at the helm, perfected the con. That the giver and not the takers got in trouble says it all about the hypocrisy of college athletics.

Everything started with the seed money from the universities and other sources. Take the 2011 Fiesta Bowl, a game between Oklahoma and unranked Connecticut. The most intriguing subplot leading into the game was just how big of a bath UConn would take for its trip, and it didn't disappoint: $1,663,560 for an athletic department that derives 26 percent of its budget from the taxpayer-funded school.

Hardest to swallow was the $2.9 million in absorbed tickets. UConn was obligated to buy 17,500 tickets, but its fans snatched up only 2,771 of those. Nearly 1,500 of UConn's allotment cost the school $255 a ticket, between five and ten times what consumers could find in the secondary ticket market. There were thousands of seats available online for $50, and plenty going for less than $20. Similar problems hit Oklahoma, forcing the Big 12 to help cover nearly $2 million worth of unsold tickets.

Never letting a dollar-making opportunity pass, the Fiesta in recent years jumped into the resale market, too. One perk of hosting the BCS championship game is the ability to package that ticket with another. Fans who wanted a seat at the Auburn–Oregon BCS championship game in 2011 were required to buy a ticket to the Fiesta Bowl, held ten days prior. For the vast majority of Auburn and Oregon fans who didn't plan on using the ticket, the Fiesta offered to resell it through a broker. When the ticket sold, the Fiesta would get a cut of those profits also. The bowl was paid twice for the same seat.

Meanwhile, the rest of the ticket market collapsed courtesy of the low-priced-seat flood. The Fiesta's practices all but guaranteed its "partner" schools would be unable to unload their overpriced seats. While the Fiesta was double dipping, Auburn and Oregon fans inclined to recoup a few bucks compromised the actual face value of the tickets. Only suckers paid face. UConn and Oklahoma were suckers 17,500 times over.

After being systematically stuck with tickets that were now nearly impossible to sell, each saw firsthand how bowls like the

Fiesta became booming businesses: Start with $7 million in guaranteed ticket sales, tack on sponsorship and TV dollars, and show minimal concern for the financial fortunes of your supposed partners.

One can hardly fault Junker for believing he was untouchable; the man figured out how to make millions on empty seats. With the largesse came Junker's insatiable need to spend: on himself, his family, his employees, their families, lawmakers, and especially those who sustained the bowl system that allowed him to pass two decades filling every hand extended to him.

Junker regularly sent brownies to Big 12 employees and cookies to one at Notre Dame. He shipped steaks to ESPN and flowers to the wife of then-Kansas athletic director Lew Perkins. Former Big East commissioner Mike Tranghese opened a set of golf clubs as a retirement present. When Junker's daughter, Lucy, applied for the honors program at Texas, Junker sent the director of the program, Jennifer Scalora, $75 worth of flowers. He billed it to the Fiesta Bowl.

For those not on Junker's personalized gift list, there was always the Fiesta Frolic, the Hope Diamond of bowl boondoggles. At the Frolic—since renamed the Fiesta Bowl Spring College Football Seminars, after athletic directors complained it sounded too disingenuous—the Fiesta offered to lodge administrators and conference commissioners, pay for two rounds of golf and two dinners, provide spa treatments for spouses, and invite guests to various hospitality suites for all sorts of primo swag. It's held at the Frank Lloyd Wright–designed Arizona Biltmore hotel—"The Jewel of the Desert," it likes to boast. The elegant resort has hosted every president since Herbert Hoover. It features two PGA-level golf courses, seven tennis courts, and eight swimming pools, including the "Catalina," which was Marilyn Monroe's favorite.

Of the eleven men on the NCAA's bowl licensing subcommittee—the group in charge of ensuring that bowls are on the up-and-up and rendering any possible punishment on the Fiesta—nine went to the Frolic in 2010. Included in that group was Mark Womack, he of the $95,000 Jack Nicklaus golf extravaganza. This is what the Cartel calls "regulators."

To expect anything else, of course, would be naïve. The Fiesta culture pervades college football. The Orange Bowl sent ADs and commissioners on their near-annual Summer Splash, a four-day Caribbean cruise that promised everything "from parasailing to sipping delicious 'Coco Locos' in a hammock."

The itinerary for the 2010 Summer Splash was obtained by the anti-BCS political action committee, PlayoffPAC. In glorious Comic Sans font it outlines a guest list, with titles included, that reads like a two-page conflict of interest: forty athletic directors—one-third of Division I-A—along with four conference commissioners and other assorted personnel.

Once they checked in on Royal Caribbean's *Majesty of the Seas* ship, with its very own Johnny Rockets, on-board casino, and rock-climbing wall, they were free to mingle about for the next four days. The Orange Bowl didn't even try to fake it: This was a shameless junket. No meetings. No planning sessions. The only responsibility was attending dinner.

"Attire: Resort Casual," the manual suggested.

Back in Phoenix, Junker eschewed Coco Locos for overpriced strip-club drinks. The $1,241.75 he spent at Bourbon Street, a Phoenix-area establishment, was expensed as "security site planning." Another Fiesta employee was reimbursed for six more trips to Bourbon Street. Junker's explanation to the panel investigating the bowl: "We are in the business where big, strong athletes are known to attend these types of establishments. It was important for us to visit, and we certainly conducted business."

For the last decade, and almost surely longer, Junker threw around his AMEX with impunity. In a 2003 performance review, the chairman of the Fiesta board told Junker to watch his expenses. Two years later, he charged $770,865 in a single year. The Fiesta expense procedure went like this: Junker turned in his entire personal credit-card bill. The bowl paid him its full amount. And then it was incumbent upon Junker to go back through and reimburse the Fiesta for all personal items.

Never mind everything the Fiesta lavished on Junker already. Of Junker's four country club memberships—two in Arizona, one in Oregon, and one in Oklahoma—none was as prized as gaining entry to the ultra-exclusive Whisper Rock in nearby Scottsdale. The club caps membership at 550, a group that boasts Phil Mickelson, Geoff Ogilvy, and Gary McCord, among other PGA Tour dignitaries. It is heaven for the golf obsessed. The Fiesta agreed to pick up Junker's $10,800-a-year membership fee as well as one for former employee Doug Boulin. It also helped Junker with the initial $100,000 entry fee by floating him an interest-free loan for the entire amount. He was supposed to pay it back in annual $10,000 installments. Instead, Junker built that amount into part of his annual raise while also including another few thousand for the taxes on the increased salary so in the end it would net him the ten grand. By the time he was fired, Junker was making nearly $700,000 a year.

The Fiesta still gave him a $27,000 annual automobile stipend (anyone know a good, reliable car you can lease for $2,250 a month?). It was part of the $84,600 spent yearly on cars for the bowl's executives. The bowl allowed Junker to purchase $31,550 worth of gold coins, which he would dole out to employees for a job he considered well done. He dropped nearly $100,000 on employee gifts over a decade. One got a $1,000 wedding bonus. Another received a $2,000 wedding bonus—for her daughter.

Some joined in on the bottomless expense account, too. One employee billed the bowl for a $1,000 bottle of wine and later 279 dozen golf balls. The Fiesta report never found out what happened to those three-thousand-plus Titleists, although one employee testified that "she had no recollection of ever seeing this large of an amount of golf balls in the office." Tack on the endless meals and drinks and so much more that reaffirmed a trope: There is no greater job than running a bowl.

If not for a mixture of hubris and paranoia, John Junker, in all likelihood, still would be doing so. Despite helping to build the Fiesta from a nothing entity into one of the BCS tent poles, Junker operated with an underdog's sense of survival. The exemplary service was to prevent the Fiesta from suffering a similar fate to the Cotton Bowl, the round of golf with Nicklaus to ingratiate his game with decision makers, the brownies and cookies to show he really, truly cares about the people.

When Junker doubted his own ability to schmooze with the power set, he hired the job out. Donnie Duncan, an old coach, athletic director, and well-connected former Big 12 commissioner, became a consultant for $4,000 a month—plus $16,000 in donations to the college saving accounts of Duncan's grandchildren. Chuck Johnson, a personable former Fiesta chairman, was paid $5,000 a month, plus first-class travel and a country club membership, to serve as a liaison between the BCS and the Fiesta Bowl. When then–Notre Dame athletic director Kevin White and his wife took a twelve-day vacation to Ireland, Johnson and his wife went along, too. The Fiesta Bowl spent $17,607.45 for that "liaison" opportunity.

Just in case those endeavors failed, Junker targeted the politicians who wielded far more influence than he ever could. The Fiesta ferried politicians on what it called "dignitary trips" around the country. One former chairman of the board said they helped the guests "learn what college football is like." The Fiesta Bowl paid the airfare, luxury hotels, meals, and game tickets for the politicians and their families. Everyone was greased sufficiently. How a game in Boston gave anyone a taste of the true college football experience was immaterial. It was an upscale city that could cater to the taste of discerning politicians. Tuscaloosa may have great football. It doesn't have the Fairmont Copley Plaza Hotel ($36,514.37 tab) or the North End's Piccolo Nido Restaurant ($5,205 dinner bill).

Junker was happy to work outside of his domain, too. He spent $4,000 on Super Bowl tickets for Ben Arredondo, a Tempe city councilman. He dropped $4,060 on Ohio State–USC seats for state senator Russell Pearce. Parking passes, suites—you name it, Junker brokered it. Only when the campaign-contribution scheme was revealed did a light shine on all of Junker's questionable spending.

On December 18, 2009, *The Arizona Republic* published a bombshell: Junker had set up a system where employees contributed money to politicians and the bowl would pay them back as bonuses. Craig Harris, an investigative reporter, had the Fiesta dead to rights: Five people who worked for the game confirmed the campaign-finance chicanery, and the story alleged tens of thousands of dollars funneled from the Fiesta coffers to politicians.

From Harris's line of questioning leading up to the story's publication, the Fiesta knew a major story was coming. Top executives tried to map out a plan in advance. They chose Grant Woods, a former Arizona attorney general, to investigate the *Republic*'s claims. Four days after the story ran, Woods told the Fiesta Bowl's executive committee members he found "no credible evidence" of reimbursement for political contributions.

They took his word.

In March 2007, a woman named Kelly Peterson married Mark Keogh in the Kansas City area. The Fiesta Bowl spent more than $13,000 on the wedding, covering everything from employees' airfare to hotel stays to rental cars to $20 worth of medicine at CVS. Peterson was John Junker's assistant, and he used his AMEX on a pair of $755.69 flights to Vancouver and another $1,189.83 for rooms at the Four Seasons there and in Whistler, British Columbia, for her honeymoon. As generously as the Fiesta Bowl treated others, it didn't skimp on its own, either.

Little did Junker realize that on a late September 2010 day, Kelly Keogh would single-handedly end his career, possibly facilitate criminal charges against him, and set in motion the revelation of bowl games' shell game. He sent Keogh to the office of Fiesta chairman of the board Duane Woods to drop off a package. She was nervous. Woods sensed something wrong. He asked if Keogh was OK. She started to talk.

The four-day investigation by Grant Woods, Keogh said, was a sham. Gary Husk, a lawyer on retainer and confidant of Junker's, had helped orchestrate a cover-up. He targeted those willing to lie, prepped their answers, and sent them in for interviews with Grant Woods. Those unwilling to go along with the ploy simply weren't asked questions. Of the $55,000 the Fiesta paid Woods, $20,000 went to Husk.

Already the Fiesta Bowl had paid Husk and his firm nearly $700,000 over the previous six years to serve as a lobbyist and consigliere. His work on the illegal contributions investigation was more covert. Keogh described a two-minute meeting with him in which he prepped her and made her feel "like you know you have to answer this way."

There was plenty to hide. According to the legitimate investigation, the Fiesta Bowl over the last decade allegedly reimbursed $46,539 to twenty-one people for campaign contributions: ten current employees, three former employees, seven spouses of current and former employees, and one volunteer.

The BCS tried to distance itself from the Fiesta. Sort of. BCS executive director Bill Hancock declared "everything in that report was disturbing" and questioned whether the bowl would keep its BCS designation. In the end, the task force allowed the Fiesta to retain its spot in the championship rotation. The chief "sanction" was forcing a $1 million donation to charities that help children in Arizona. Of course, the task force could've just told the Fiesta to follow its own legally binding articles of incorporation, which declare all profits (an estimated $10 million-plus in fiscal 2011) go to charity. If anything, the so-called sanction saved the bowl millions. This wasn't a slap on the wrist; it was a pat on the back.

Meanwhile, Hancock continued to praise the Frolic as a "remarkable business opportunity" and defended his own acceptance of gifts and golf. He didn't take up Giannini, the Southern Miss athletic director, on his offer to resign from the BCS task force looking into the Fiesta.

Hancock didn't ask the Orange Bowl or Sugar Bowl or any of the other bowls with similar non-itemized expenditures, executive salaries, and profit margins to undergo the same level of scrutiny as the Fiesta Bowl report. All they submitted was a thin explanation of their business practices that went unchallenged. He didn't take issue with other bowl games doling out gifts and services to college administrators in the same "disturbing" fashion as the Fiesta. To do so was to risk finding out that while the Fiesta's excess might be an outlier, its practices surely aren't.

"You can't indict the entire bowl system because of what's gone on out there," NCAA president Mark Emmert said. "My hope is that it will also serve as a warning shot that every community that runs a bowl game makes sure they're doing the oversight compliance and due diligence to make sure their bowl games are well run."

Idealism dripped from Emmert's words. It's wonderful to think that bowls suddenly will turn conscientious, that they'll stop taking from schools, that those in charge of athletic departments will adhere to ethical boundaries. By now, he ought to know better. The next John Junker is out there somewhere with an AMEX, an inflated sense of self, and millions of university dollars burning a hole in his pocket.

 High-Paid Blazers

The bowl system is ripe for financial abuse. Despite enjoying nonprofit status, there is plenty of profit. Much of it, in fact, ends up back in people's pockets. The same people who aid and abet the Cartel in its defiling of college football. There is no other way to explain how bowl executives haul in outrageous salaries when their entire year revolves around preparing for one game. Some schools stage as many as eight home games a season, and they certainly don't pay their operations directors half a million dollars.

And yet that's nearly how much Rick Baker, the executive director of the Cotton Bowl, received in compensation for 2007, according to tax records. Baker made $490,433, and that doesn't include fringe benefits, transportation, travel, and a healthy expense account. He's not the only one getting fat on bowls, either. Nearly two dozen bowl executives received more than $300,000 in total compensation, according to federal tax filings. Outback Bowl president Jim McVay was paid $808,032 in fiscal 2008 and $693,212 in 2009. Sugar Bowl CEO Paul Hoolahan pocketed $645,386. John Junker of the Fiesta totaled $673,888 (plus the aforementioned limitless AMEX). Alamo Bowl CEO Derrick Fox took in $419,045. The Chick-fil-A Bowl in Atlanta sent $1.15 million in salary and benefits to the local chamber of commerce that oversees the game.

"Why does the executive director of the Cotton Bowl get almost a half a million dollars a year to stage a one-week series of events that culminate in an exhibition football game?" Rep. Joe Barton said. "I would've thought they had volunteers who do most of that, and they paid the executive director $60,000 or $75,000 to answer the mail and attend chamber events."

Barton is not one to complain about salaries. Rank-and-file members of the United States House of Representatives enjoy an annual salary of $174,000, which puts them in the top 10 percent of all earners in America. Barton repeatedly acknowledges how lucky he is. He simply can't fathom what constitutes an income near $500,000 for running a football game when the participating teams pay their own way and sell their own tickets, and an army of unpaid workers do the executive director's bidding. Neither, it seems, could Baker. He took a pay cut in 2008 and made only $356,154 to manage the same one game. A raise in 2009 bumped him back to $470,147.

It's not like Baker is some entrepreneur who started the thing. The Cotton Bowl is in its seventy-sixth year, and if seven decades have proven anything, it's that bowl games might as well be licenses to spin gold. While fledgling games regularly used to go out of business, the revenue that filters toward bowls today practically acts as a failsafe.

"Maybe I should switch jobs and run one of these bowls," Barton said, and he's got a point: Running a bowl may be the cushiest gig there is. Bowls expanded rapidly for a reason, and only a three-year moratorium has kept them from growing beyond the current thirty-five. As long as bowls make decisions with money in mind, someone new will want to hop aboard.

The salaries are extraordinary, and it doesn't take a major bowl to rake in money. The Emerald Bowl, a lower-tier game in San Francisco since renamed the Kraft Fight Hunger Bowl, was small-time by bowl standards in 2009, totaling $3.4 million in expenditures. About 11.2 percent of the game's spending went into the pocket of executive director Gary Cavalli, and the $377,475 in salary did not include benefits or other accoutrements.

The IRS has statutes governing nonprofit spending, and that includes executive pay. Bowls say they are compliant because the pay rates compare with similar nonprofits. Which ones? Other bowl games, naturally. Marcus S. Owens, who headed the IRS's Exempt Organizations Division for ten years, believes otherwise. On behalf of PlayoffPAC, the political action committee whose anti-BCS vigor helped spur governmental intervention, Owens signed a formal complaint in 2010 asking the IRS to examine bowl spending on compensation, and prohibited lobbying and other misuse of funds. The IRS does not comment on possible cases, although it doesn't shy away from taking on high-profile nonprofits, especially in times when governments are running huge deficits.

Bowl executives often make more than their local college athletic directors, a position with far greater demands and responsibilities. The executive director of the New Orleans Area Habitat for Humanity, who spearheaded construction for people displaced by Hurricane Katrina, was paid $97,500 in fiscal 2009, according to tax records—about 15 percent of what the Sugar Bowl CEO received.

Research done by PlayoffPAC showed that the average CEO pay for nonprofits with comparable budgets ($10 million to $25 million) is $185,270. In 2008, the Outback's McVay received almost four and half times that. In many cases, bowl CEO salaries keep soaring, even as the rest of the country—and especially the universities they do business with—is struggling. The Sugar Bowl's Hoolahan was paid $451,674 in 2007. Two years later he was making nearly $200,000 more, a 42.9 percent raise. His top assistant's pay was up 36.6 percent. Junker's compensation jumped 24 percent from 2007 to 2009. And why did McVay manage to make over $800,000 that one year? He picked up a retention bonus of $112,000, according to CBSSports.com. Retention bonus? Did the Outback Bowl really fear someone would quit a $600,000-plus-per-year job operating a second-tier bowl game?

Of course, running a bowl isn't simple. It is, in many cases, very simple. It's not far-fetched to suggest that just about anyone with minimal game-management experience could sell out the Georgia Dome for a New Year's Eve game between a local school (Georgia Tech) and the defending national champion (Louisiana State). That was the 2008 Chick-fil-A Bowl: a true open-the-doors, print-the-tickets, and count-the-cash night.

How the Chick-fil-A operates takes neither a quantum physicist nor a pathologist to understand. Its M.O. is simple enough for a business-school dropout: exploit a cushy date and time (New Year's Eve) and broadcast partner (ESPN), and invite two nearby teams that will sell reams of tickets. The low-hanging fruit is sweetest to the Chick-fil-A Bowl, on-field competitiveness be damned. All the hullabaloo from the Cartel about how the regular season means everything and needs to be guarded at all costs simply isn't important to bowl directors, who favor proximity and passion more than actual results.

This is the system the Cartel fights for: one in which most bowl executives, clad in their garish blazers, personally pocket hundreds of thousands of dollars while turning college football's postseason into a revenue-grabbing free-for-all. You can fault the bowl directors only so much. They are businessmen getting what they can from a bureaucracy that invites them to pilfer. They've found a willing partner, in part because increasingly, the athletic director who is supposed to guard his school's money gets a cut of the action, too.

Reaching a bowl game isn't difficult for any team, and it's particularly easy for a school from one of the big six conferences (and major independent Notre Dame). During the 2009–10 bowl season, forty-six of the sixty-six teams from those leagues (69.7 percent) went to a game. Many of the appearances were money losers that required schools to use conference revenue sharing to cover the loss.

"The fact we didn't go to a bowl game the last two years means we actually made money," former Michigan AD Bill Martin said in 2010, trying to find the only bright side of the Wolverines' recent struggles.

In most businesses, blowing the company's resources is cause for dismissal. Athletic directors have convinced their presidents that this isn't just a positive but cause for a sizeable merit bonus.

Nowhere else could employees trick their bosses into thinking that avoiding the bottom 30 percent of their professional peer group warrants a five-figure pop. And yet Missouri athletic director Mike Alden receives an extra month's pay ($23,947.92) if the Tigers go to even the lowliest bowl game. Oregon's Rob Mullens picks up a $50,000 bonus for any bowl appearance by the Ducks. When Kentucky went to the lowly BBVA Compass Bowl and spent $276,740 over allotment, AD Mitch Barnhart received $30,000. North Carolina's Dick Baddour earns $24,583.33. These are just a few examples among many; any AD who doesn't get big money for a small bowl needs a new agent.

For agreeing to that lopsided 2009 Fiesta Bowl deal—in which Ohio State spent $1.7 million in travel and entertainment costs, wasted $1 million on empty seats, and went $820,000 over the Big Ten's expense allowance, according to university records—Buckeyes athletic director Gene Smith picked up a $54,000 bonus. It was hardly a harmless, easily recovered, cost-of-doing-business expenditure. Smith soon thereafter announced he was raising football and men's basketball ticket prices, plus fees at the school golf course, to help offset a projected revenue shortfall. John Junker's Fiesta Bowl, flush with the Buckeyes' money, had no such budgetary concerns.

Even some assistant ADs and other mid-level staffers are in on the deal. At Virginia Tech, the director and assistant director of the school band get $4,000 and $2,000, respectively, for any bowl trip. Sure, it might make financial sense for the school to decline a sure loser of a bowl invite, but then none of the bosses would get their year-end bump.

Let's be clear on the scam that's going on here: Lower-tier bowls exist solely because athletic directors are willing to lose their employers' money to prop the games up. There is no bowl game without the university's open checkbook to buy tickets they won't sell and blowing through cash on other expenses. Yet the ADs have persuaded their employers to handsomely reward them for going to an event that wouldn't exist without the school.

It's little wonder so many ADs argue to protect the current system and gleefully blow big money so games can remain in business. Or that almost no AD ever turns down a bowl invite, preferring to wax on about the intangible benefits of the appearance. It's even less surprising that the number of bowl games keeps growing, or that the Big 12 pushed through a rule change that allows bowl games to select a 6-6 team from a power conference ahead of a team with a superior record from another league. There's even talk of petitioning the NCAA to deem 5-7 teams bowl eligible.

Critics contend that the proliferation of bowl games is college football's version of participation trophies. Everyone's a winner. The Cartel cackles at such innocence. Forget the trophy; just cut the check.

Understanding the compromised position of the athletic director on the other side of the bargaining table, bowl directors are so comfortable with their place that they don't bother denying their motivation is straight profit.

Ken Hoffman was the sports information director at Michigan State until 1997, when he teamed with former Spartans coach George Perles and created the Motor City Bowl in metro Detroit. With its slot in the bowl calendar a day or two after Christmas, it became an immediate punch line. Who, exactly, wanted to spend Christmas in Detroit?

Fans of the Mid-American Conference living in Michigan or Ohio, it turned out, had no problem with the Motor City Bowl. After a few years of tinkering, Hoffman found the proper formula for profit, matching a MAC team against a national program desperate for any bowl scraps. Occasionally, he even lures a Big Ten team.

The game draws about 40,000-plus fans annually and enjoys an ESPN deal. When the American auto industry collapsed, killing sponsorship from Detroit's automakers, Hoffman got local pizza magnate Mike Ilitch to come aboard and rebrand the game the Little Caesar's Pizza Bowl. Even in a city beset by unemployment and desolation, a bowl of minor import didn't just survive; it thrived.

Hoffman doesn't hide behind his motivation: He wants to sell tickets. It's why he focuses on local teams. He'll happily take two MAC teams if they'll draw a crowd. Any mediocre team from the state of Michigan might as well book its trip to Detroit. In 2008, Hoffman had a choice of the MAC's champion, Buffalo, or a 12-1 Ball State team that spent most of the season in the national polls and was on the cusp of cracking the BCS before losing the conference championship. Instead, the bowl invited a Central Michigan team that wound up losing three straight games to end the season. It was the only school with a big enough alumni base in Detroit to ensure ticket sales.

Though the game still draws snickers, Hoffman took it private at the turn of the century and has since expanded his company. He ran the International Bowl in Toronto for three years and said he would start another game if he could secure the proper conference tie-ins. Forget size. Even the smallest bowl game can be a hugely profitable venture.

The system ensures so. Not only do schools support bowl games with crazy ticket guarantees, but they treat the bowl representatives like royalty. Consider the infamous bowl scouts, relics from a bygone era that persist today despite their patent uselessness. In the 1970s, when few regular-season games were televised and bowls actually tried to piece together attractive matchups—not just schools that would agree to tickets in lieu of payout—they would send talent evaluators to figure out whether a team was a worthwhile candidate.

Since there were only about a dozen bowl games, the selection committees could be choosy. Schools responded by wining and dining the scout in an effort to win goodwill and garner a coveted bid. Bowl scouts were lavished with prime hotel rooms in town, the best parking spots at the stadium, and tickets with press box and sideline access. The school president might throw a private cocktail party for them. Bowl scouts mattered, even if their mission and skills were dubious.

Little, in that respect, has changed. Every week, a herd of bowl scouts—these days often cronies of the game's executive director—scatters across the country living a fan's dream life. Scouts can see Oklahoma–Texas one week and Notre Dame–USC another, and it's all for free—or, at least, at the expense of the bowl game and university.

"I call them the March of the Entitled," said a major college assistant athletic director, who for years has spent Friday nights throwing parties for bowl scouts. "They show up and want their ass kissed, steak, and Scotch. Every single weekend we have to entertain these guys, and they aren't even scouting; they're just here for a good time. I've been arguing for years we stop, but no one will."

Often the scouting trips are wildly impractical or thinly veiled attempts to score free tickets to the game of the week. The Chick-fil-A, for instance, scouts as many as nine games a weekend, often sending two people. A DirecTV hook-up and a roomful of TVs could offer the same perspective at a fraction of the price.

For its 2007 game, the Sugar Bowl spent $272,231 on its selection committee, even though, as a BCS game, its choice was obvious. The Sugar Bowl picked LSU against Notre Dame, snagging the local team for ticket sales and the nation's biggest TV draw for a deeper impact. Not a single scout needed to see a single snap all season for Sugar Bowl brass to pair the Tigers and the Irish.

In 2009, when No. 3 Alabama hosted No. 9 LSU, a rep from the Papajohns.com Bowl showed up at Bryant-Denny Stadium. Either a bowl game that wound up with two unranked 7-5 teams actually considered the possibility of landing a top 10 SEC powerhouse, or somebody was jonesing for a trip to Tuscaloosa. If, by some accident of nature, Alabama was available, no bowl scout was needed to inform the blazers that the Crimson Tide was indeed worthy of a pizza bowl berth.

With a playoff, perhaps the lifestyle gets reined in and bowls learn a thing or two about financial pragmatism. The ones who suffer the most are the Cartel's leeching bowl executives, who will learn quickly that they can't suck their games dry without consequences. If other fat gets cut, suddenly the half-million-dollar salaries could be scrutinized.

Imagine the Kraft Fight Hunger Bowl—the little game that could, with its title sponsor vowing to help solve one of the nation's most endemic issues—assessing Gary Cavalli's salary and wondering how one person really deserves nearly 11 percent of the company's revenue. It's plenty more equitable to halve that, in which case Cavalli would make $188,737 to run a semi-anonymous football game that takes place once a year.

In other words, he'd be paid like a mere United States congressman.

7 Presidential Problem

Harvey Perlman is the chancellor of the University of Nebraska-Lincoln. He's a learned man, an accomplished lawyer who spends his days trying to figure out how to run an institution that earns prestigious Carnegie Research status. He also previously served as the chair of the BCS Presidential Oversight Committee, a job perfect for someone like Perlman.

But Perlman does not understand football. He can't. Because no Nebraska-born, Nebraska-raised, Nebraska-educated, and, for more than three decades, Nebraska-employed person would do what Perlman did: laugh at the viability of a playoff with on-campus games. In rejecting the possibility of postseason football at legendary venues such as Nebraska's Memorial Stadium, Perlman gives the impression that, well, Nebraska stinks.

"You're . . . going to have to play at home sites—which I'm sure everybody will want to play in Nebraska in December and January," he told the *Nebraska State Paper* with a heavy sheen of sarcasm. Which was met by an equal dose of scorn, since the truth is, yeah, the prospect of a game in Nebraska in December and January *does* thrill just about everybody.

Nebraska fans, for example, wouldn't oppose watching their Cornhuskers in some of the most important games ever staged in the legendary stadium. Better that than traveling to some dull municipal facility for a bowl game in an unfamiliar place that doesn't carry the smell of Runza meat pies and Big Red hot dogs, staples of Nebraska home games.

And surely the out-of-town fans and television viewers would love seeing the blizzard of red that fills the famed 81,067-seat stadium. The Heisman and Outland trophy displays, the statue of Tom Osborne, the Blackshirt defense—college football enthusiasts appreciate history and tradition, and Nebraska teems with both as much as any school.

Nebraska players and coaches would cherish the chance, too. Games in front of a partisan crowd filled with friends and family. The opportunity to finally see how those SEC teams handle an icy field and bone-chilling winds. The prospect of riding home-field advantage, the reward for a superlative regular season, to a national championship.

Most of all, the people to whom Perlman should answer, his students and faculty, reap the benefits. In a time of budget cuts and soaring tuition, Nebraska—and every college and university in the country, for that matter—could use the millions of dollars a playoff would send its way.

And better yet, it would pour money back into the city of Lincoln. If regular-season games are a boon, imagine the playoffs, with increased out-of-town media, higher ticket prices, and an even more hyped atmosphere. Hotels, restaurants, bars, grocery stores, parking garages, and the university would all swim in cash. Apparently, Perlman is more interested in filling the coffers of some town in Florida or Texas with Nebraskans' money.

"We would love a [playoff] game here," said Wendy Birdsall, president of the Lincoln Chamber of Commerce. "I'm an economic developer. I'm all for looking for opportunities for the community and bringing in revenue."

What, then, is Perlman's rationale to scoff at his university's destination stadium, his community's need for economic stimulus, and the chance to market Nebraska's flagship campus? Certainly it can't be the weather, as Perlman subtly alludes. You can't argue against snowflakes, which have kissed some of football's greatest games. All weather is football weather, and only a suit drunk on talking points would try to rationalize otherwise. The best game-day experience in the NFL is at Lambeau Field in Green Bay, Wisconsin, a town smaller and colder than Lincoln. It hosted perhaps the most famous football game in history: the 1967 Ice Bowl between the Green Bay Packers and Dallas Cowboys, in which the game-time wind chill was 48 degrees below zero.

Perlman makes the same mistake as all the other university presidents who align themselves with an economically underperforming system that robs fans and players: Rather than look into the BCS himself, Perlman bases his opinion almost exclusively on the very people who profit from it.

"Most presidents don't know what is going on with the BCS," said Charles Young, the former president of the University of Florida and chancellor of UCLA. "If they did, they wouldn't allow it. They are being led around by their conference commissioners."

It's easy to explain. Perlman has a busy university to run. So presidents ask their conference commissioners for their take and listen to the bowl representatives who wine and dine them every December during bowl trips. Armed with the party line, they fight blindly.

In November 2010, Ohio State president E. Gordon Gee made national waves when he argued that schools from major conferences deserve a spot in the BCS title game over teams from perceived lesser conference—in this instance, TCU and Boise State.

"We do not play the Little Sisters of the Poor," Gee told the Associated Press. "So I think until a university runs through that gauntlet that there's some reason to believe that they not be the best teams to [be] in the big ballgame."

Doctors almost resorted to surgery to help remove Gee's foot from his mouth. Why a university president would, without provocation, bash another school's student-athletes was beyond the pale. Various rating systems showed TCU and Boise State's schedules to be comparable or superior to that of Ohio State, which had played a lackluster nonconference slate. Overwhelmed with criticism, Gee repeatedly apologized. When TCU defeated Big Ten member Wisconsin in the Rose Bowl to cap off an undefeated season, Gee said he would order crow at dinner that night.

"I need to keep my mouth shut," he told *The Columbus Dispatch*. "What do I know about college football? I look like Orville Redenbacher. I have no business talking about college football."

That may be true. Unfortunately, Gee also positioned himself as among the chief proponents of the BCS and a roadblock to change, once declaring "They'll have to wrench a playoff system from my cold, dead hands." That sort of leadership from a man with "no business talking about college football."

"There were folks who really were rallied in a way [that] I'm sure President Gee had no intention of rallying them," Boise State president Bob Kustra said. "Even if you are an Illini or a Badger, there's no question you can see through some of the pitfalls and the perils of this current system."

Actually, Gee's instincts on strength of schedule weren't entirely wrong. His understanding of the BCS and how a potential playoff would work posed the problem. Gee was smart enough to realize that just because a team finishes undefeated, it shouldn't automatically leapfrog ahead of a one-loss squad with a more arduous schedule. You need not know anything about college football to understand that an arbitrary system based on false premises and misguided groupthink is wrong. A one-loss Big Ten team had a good argument to be ranked ahead of unbeaten TCU. Gee's confusion was that in defending the BCS, he was actually debunking it.

The issue was simple: Had Oregon or Auburn lost a regular-season game in 2010, the BCS was prepared to put TCU in the title game thanks mostly to its perfect record, according to BCS analyst Jerry Palm. (A one-loss Auburn team would've had a 50-50 chance of staying in front of TCU, Palm said, although the backlash from the Cam Newton scandal may have doomed the Tigers.) Since TCU had reached No. 3 in the BCS standings, if either Oregon or Auburn had dropped out of the top two there was little chance a one-loss, major-conference team could climb over it. Would an unbeaten TCU deserve a title-game slot over one-loss major-conference teams? Maybe, maybe not. It's debatable. To Gee, the answer was an unequivocal no, an opinion shared by plenty of fair-minded fans.

One problem: Gee continues to defend the system that came perilously close to unleashing his nightmare scenario. If he was troubled by the concept of TCU in the title game, he was troubled by the BCS. He wraps his cold, dead hands around his ideological opposite because years of falsehoods have programmed him to think that way, and Gee never realized it.

Just like Perlman, he trusted the Cartel and became a stooge for the system. A well-hewn anti-playoff excuse is that "the presidents" are against a playoff. Well, no one in the BCS presents them with a viable playoff option. Perlman, whose career as a lawyer was rooted in the logic of an argument, otherwise would not believe that Lincoln is unworthy of hosting a football game. The Cartel does not dare educate the educators. Finding naïve university leaders such as Perlman to serve as spokesmen is one of its most brilliant ideas.

"The ones who get involved aren't reformers," said Andrew Zimbalist, a sports economist and expert on college athletics. "They're jock sniffers. They're passionate about their sports and have fun. They're not going to push for any major change. They're representing conferences, and the conferences wouldn't let them sit there if they thought they were going to change the system."

As the attacks on the BCS intensified from the halls of Congress to online chat rooms and every imaginable forum for public ridicule, the Cartel realized it needed more people to take the blame. Preferably some with more clout. So in 2003, the men who hold college football hostage turned to the men in the ivory towers and formed the Presidential Oversight Committee.

The 120 school presidents and chancellors offered authority, credentials, and brainpower. They were, in theory, academics who would ensure that athletic departments served their schools and not the other way around. Turns out they were pawns.

Predictably, they cited missed classes as one of the key reasons a playoff wouldn't work. Never mind that the three lower divisions of college football run playoffs in the middle of finals and still post graduation rates higher than Division I-A. Major-conference presidents were polled for a 2009 thesis by James Madison University graduate student Thomas Deary, and among their top three oppositions to a playoff was the concern that "student-athletes would miss additional classes." Perlman was one of the presidents who voted that way. In a statement read before a Senate Judiciary Subcommittee on Antitrust Issues, Perlman further expressed concerns about a playoff "interfering with the academic calendar or impinging on the academic missions of our universities."

Perlman and his fellow presidents gleefully cash checks from college basketball, which requires exponentially more missed class time. And they relentlessly expand their conferences, with travel increasing likewise—in Nebraska's case, joining the thousand-mile-wide Big Ten in 2011. And at the University of Alabama, they closed the entire school for three days due to the 2010 BCS title game. Yes, the entire school. For the 2011 BCS championship game, Oregon players missed over a week of classes. Not to actually play the game but to hang around Arizona and promote it through daily media sessions.

Perlman clearly didn't think about the issue before taking a position. Organizers could conduct an entire sixteen-team playoff in the current time span it takes to put on thirty-five bowl games. Most, if not all, games would take place during semester break. The missed-class-time argument is so specious—"That's just crap," Mountain West commissioner Craig Thompson said—even the Cartel can't stand by it.

"The academic effect, it's just not a credible argument," Big Ten commissioner Jim Delany said. "I think some of the arguments that have been advanced against the playoffs have not been credible."

The Cartel would know. It authors most of them. And because its members so excel at being a moving target, no one person or group is ever responsible for the failures of the BCS. It's the presidents. The bowls. The athletic directors. The computers. The voters. The Cartel always dreams up another scapegoat. If it can cast blame toward another part of its group, the standard is safe. It's Bureaucracy Survival 101. For years, four conference commissioners passed around the role of BCS coordinator in order to share the slings and arrows tossed by the public. In 2009, they got sick of it and hired a public relations man, Bill Hancock, regarded as one of the nicest and most polite men in college sports, to do it for them.

While Hancock took the fancy title of executive director and embraced his role as public dartboard, it didn't keep Perlman from giving the old college try. If he happens to trash his own state and argue against his university's best interests, so be it. The Cartel intended nothing less.

The more people who oppose the idea of on-campus playoff

games, the better. It allows the perpetuation of another red herring: that a playoff would have to include bowl games as hosts. It's a key argument to making a playoff seem unworkable, because there is little doubt that trying to stage a three- or four-week, neutral-site tournament would cause prohibitive travel costs and, consequently, half-empty stadiums.

But it's an argument built around a false premise—the assumption that a playoff-bowl marriage is the best option, which it decidedly isn't. A playoff doesn't have to use bowl games as neutral sites. Play the first three rounds on campus and let the bowls operate on their own outside the system.

By using campus sites until the playoff championship game, every stadium would sell out. Home fans would gobble up any unused tickets by the visiting team, and the revenues would grow exponentially. The NCAA's lower divisions and NFL each use home sites in their playoffs. The Cartel ignores this and laughably argues that Division I-AA and II and III games don't sell out. Hancock even cited the mediocre home playoff crowds at the University of Montana as an example, as if it's in any way similar to the sport's highest level. USC visiting Alabama would cause Bryant-Denny Stadium to sell out before the opening guitar riff of "Sweet Home Alabama" was complete. And that's just one of a hundred tremendous games a playoff could provide.

In its manipulation of the presidents, the Cartel has taken Lenin's old edict—a lie told often enough becomes the truth—to a new level. A lie told often enough by a Ph.D. sounds even more truthful. There's a reason so many proposed playoffs by fans and media still include using the bowl sites.

Not even the Cartel can come up with an argument for the antiseptic stadiums used at most bowls over the dozens of historic stadiums with stirring game-day environments. In their place, the Cartel offers a menagerie of dull, money-draining spots that, outside of the Rose Bowl, Sun Bowl, and a few other select stadiums, can't compete with any big-time college experience. The Citrus Bowl's grass surface was so poor for two 2009–10 bowl games that *Orlando Sentinel* columnist Mike Bianchi decried "the deplorable state of our garbage dump football stadium and the cesspool we call a playing field." No one ever wrote that about Memorial Stadium.

Leaders of self-respecting sports organizations laugh at how the bowl system works. Imagine telling NFL commissioner Roger Goodell he should take a second look at the 2011 AFC Championship game. It was played in Pittsburgh, where Steelers fans ensured a sold-out, multimillion-dollar gate. The Steelers owned the state-of-the-art building, pocketed the parking and concession money, and allowed the league to control all sponsorship rights and television revenue.

Anyone who suggested moving the game to the Citrus Bowl, where a promoter in Orlando gets up to 60 percent of the money the game generates and then puts the NFL on the hook for all travel costs, would get thrown out of Goodell's Manhattan office. Not only does the Cartel consider this a positive arrangement, it regards the thievery as an institution.

Then it sends its minions to preach the virtues of the BCS. If Perlman bothered to listen to his coconspirators, perhaps he would understand that in backing them he takes money out of his hometown's pocket.

During his 2009 testimony in front of Congress, Alamo Bowl CEO Derrick Fox equated playoff proponents to zealots who would rob cities of the money generated by bowl games. "They neither know nor care about the fact that those billions— yes, billions—of dollars of economic impact are generated by the existing system," Fox said.

Fox, on the other hand, neither knows nor cares that those

billions—yes, billions—have "zero economic impact" on the American economy. It's true. Just read the 2007 Valero Alamo Bowl Economic & Fiscal Impact Analysis, the very study Fox commissioned and quoted to come up with his billion-dollar figure. Fox tried to use the report, which detailed spending by out-of-town fans at San Antonio area hotels and restaurants, as the foundation for his argument. Beyond Fox's cherry-picking, the study actually ended up proving moot the Cartel's entire theory on economic impact.

When on Capitol Hill, Fox failed to mention a concept in the report called "displaced spending," which declares local fans are far less valuable to bowl cities than tourists because locals would have spent their entertainment dollar elsewhere in the city.

There's no doubt about the value of out-of-town fans to local businesses. They bring money earned outside the city into it, enriching the overall economy. Local fans are different. While some San Antonians drop $100 going to the Alamo Bowl, they provide no economic impact because if there were no Alamo Bowl, they would've spent the $100 on some other business in San Antonio—a restaurant across town or at the mall on a major purchase. The money spent on the game is money not spent elsewhere.

"Most spending by local residents is considered to be displaced spending and is not counted as part of economic impact," the Alamo Bowl study said. "[The local fan] is, therefore, providing zero economic impact."

The true economic impact of bowl games depends on the size of the economy being studied. The Alamo Bowl can brag to the mayor of San Antonio about the money out-of-town visitors contribute to the local economy. If the majority of the tourists came from, say, Houston, Fox wouldn't dare be so effusive with the governor of Texas, to whom money spent in San Antonio is the same as money spent in Houston. A $100 net gain for San Antonio is a $100 net loss for Houston and zero sum for the state of Texas.

Accordingly, Fox's own study discredits the displaced-spending argument he proffered in front of Congress. By citing the revenue of all bowls, he groups them together nationally. On that scale, all spending is displaced spending, all Americans locals. Thus, the billion dollars cited in the study is, according to its own displaced-spending theory, "providing zero economic impact"—and the Cartel pulled off a neat trick: immolating its very own argument.

Using the 2010 Alamo Bowl as an example, there is no value for the American economy in taking money from Michigan State fans and putting it in Texas. Having Michigan State fans eat at a San Antonio Applebee's is no different than having them eat at an East Lansing Applebee's—except for San Antonio and East Lansing. If the Cartel wants to cite the billion dollars of economic impact for some communities, it must mention the billion dollars sucked out of the economies in other communities. And to really get technical, bowl games likely had a negative impact on the American economy. For three years, the International Bowl was played in Toronto. With few, if any, foreign tourists coming to watch games in the United States, bowls, as a whole, may have taken money out of the country.

Then there is this: "When did our job as a university become supporting the hospitality industry in certain states?" asked West Virginia athletic director Oliver Luck. He's troubled by the concept that schools are lucky to break even or turn a small profit because it's a "bowl game" when they'd never do that for a regular-season contest. "Football is an economic engine at every Division I school," Luck said. "You need a strong and successful football program to pay the bill. We have a limited number of games. When we put the Mountaineer football team on the field, it has to be a profit center."

Economic-impact studies cited by bowls and professional sports leagues, often boasting of hundreds of millions of dollars brought into the local economy, have long been debunked by academics and independent research. Scores of investigations have shown that the studies repeatedly offer inflated results designed to aid the arguments of event organizers, politicians, and owners who seek public financing of stadiums.

"They only count the good and then multiply it by two or three," said Philip Porter, a professor of economics at the University of South Florida. Some studies assume a hotel or restaurant will be empty if not for the event and then take credit for every customer. Or they don't acknowledge that much of the actual profit from major hotels, car-rental agencies, and even in some instances chain restaurants immediately leaves town to far-off corporate headquarters. While positives accompany fans visiting town, Porter said, "the economic impact on a local economy is almost always overstated."

It's an increasingly dubious concept anyway. Bowl executives now prefer to invite teams with local fan bases to their games. North Carolina went to the Meineke Car Care Bowl in Charlotte in 2008 and 2009. Hawaii played in the Hawaii Bowl in 2008 and 2010. The Humanitarian Bowl in Boise selected Idaho in 2009. The 2010 Poinsettia Bowl featured nearby San Diego State. The local fans deemed less valuable by the Cartel actually anchor ticket sales and stabilize bowl revenue, economic impact be damned. Bowl executives have prioritized their own revenue from ticket sales over what communities gain from tourists.

For the 2008–09 bowl season, more than a third of the games

featured a local school. Eight were from the host city or a short drive from it, and four others came from within a three-hour drive or were in-state schools. In 2009–10, nine bowl games fell into those categories. For 2010–11, it was up to fourteen—relative home games 40 percent of the time. Having the University of Florida play at the Outback Bowl in Tampa, home to plenty of local fans and just a two-hour drive from Gainesville, didn't fill hotel rooms for a week. The majority of UF fans were either locals or folks that drove in the afternoon of the game and fled right after.

It also doesn't do much for one of the Cartel's talking points: the "cultural experience" of a bowl trip. The Gators in Tampa, a cultural experience? Texas A&M in suburban Dallas? Tennessee in Nashville? San Diego State, Hawaii, and SMU played bowl games in their home stadiums. "I did not want to be in Dallas for Christmas," SMU tackle Kevin Beachum told the *Dallas Morning News* about the Mustangs' trip across campus for the Bell Helicopter Armed Forces Bowl.

The Music City Bowl showed little concern for Nashville's economic impact in 2009 by inviting Vanderbilt, whose campus sits three miles from the game's home, LP Field. The Motor City Bowl didn't select Central Michigan three consecutive years to produce a renaissance for Detroit. Southeastern Michigan houses the Chippewas' largest alumni base. The Las Vegas Bowl chose Brigham Young five consecutive years, from 2005 to 2009, because Cougars fans travel in large numbers from nearby Utah and buy tickets. It's certainly not to provide a boon for the Strip, with the majority of Mormon fans teetotaling non-gamblers.

In 2010, the game branched out. It took Utah.

"I think bowls' business models have changed," said Gary Stokan, president of the Chick-fil-A Bowl, which in 2009 invited Georgia Tech, situated just over a mile from the Georgia Dome.

"When we all originally started, bowls were created to really develop economic impact. That's still our goal. But with the contracted payouts you have now, you've got to weigh that, balance the economic-impact figure with attendance."

Which means the local economic impact about which Fox boasted to Congress—"supporting pre- and post-Christmas business in hotels, restaurants, and visitor attractions," he said— is not just nationally nonexistent; plenty of bowls don't care about it.

Even after Delany dismissed the academic reasoning and Stokan brought proper perspective to economic-impact fabrication, Perlman repeated the BCS boilerplate at the subcommittee hearing on July 7, 2009. He mentioned academics. He mentioned the financial impact for bowl communities. He mentioned the impossibility of staging a playoff at bowl locations. He went down the dirty laundry list of excuses.

And no one stopped or corrected Perlman, leaving him open to even more criticism. The Cartel would let him take the flak. It knew a good, naïve mouthpiece when it saw one.

Myth of the Dead Bowls

Fear-mongering is an area of particular expertise for the Cartel. When comparing a playoff with the BCS, it loses the debate over excitement, fairness, and profit, so like a desperate politician interested in shifting the focus of a campaign, it goes negative. And in doing so, the Cartel tells perhaps its biggest lie of all: With a playoff system, bowl games would vanish.

"We believe the bowl system wouldn't survive a playoff," BCS executive director Bill Hancock said.

"The bowl season is dead," Big Ten commissioner Jim Delany warned in *USA Today*. "Dead."

Dead? An entire month of games wiped from existence? Some critics wouldn't care if a half-dozen of the smaller games did expire. That's not us. If two teams want to play a college football game, we're all for it, so long as the games aren't financially pillaging the participants. Bowl games are fun to play in, watch, and attend. Nobody wants to see the Rose Bowl die, which is why the Cartel claims that playoff proponents want to stick a knife through the heart of Pasadena.

A thorough analysis of the industry shows that the dead-bowl theory is simply another Cartel myth. Bowls would continue to operate in the shadow of a playoff. Undoubtedly. The good times and good games can roll on, only without holding the sport hostage by blocking the creation of the playoff. If the question is playoff or bowls, the answer is both. The proof is in the way bowls operate fiscally and the real monetary impact of a playoff on college athletics. To move past the hysteria planted by the Cartel, we studied the available financial statements, tax filings, and business plans of private and nonprofit bowl games and spoke with numerous bowl executives, television deal makers, athletic directors, governors, private businessmen, and conference commissioners.

The conclusion: If you love bowl games (as we do) and want to see them played for decades to come (as we do), you wouldn't oppose a playoff. You would fight for it.

The Cartel originally claimed every bowl would be wiped out—the major BCS games, the mid-tier ones, and, of course, the fledgling small events. Hancock later amended that, saying "some" would survive. Actually, all would.

Take the absurd implication that the Rose Bowl couldn't survive a playoff. With the game's brand, rich history, and coveted late-afternoon New Year's Day television spot—none of which would go away with a playoff—the best lawyer in the world couldn't make a case against it thriving. The game wouldn't get two conference champions, but it would still feature two major schools with huge fan bases thrilled to attend the most storied game in college football. For the January 1, 2010, game, that could've meant Penn State–Oregon State rather than Ohio State–Oregon.

The Rose Bowl's $30-million-a-year TV contract may dip in value, but a panel of four television executives interviewed for this book said it would remain at least a $15 million to $20 million property on top of selling a hundred thousand tickets and raking in parking, title sponsorship, advertising, and concessions. Right now, it's a $51-million-a-year event, according to federal tax records, and the man who for the last decade ran the

Rose Bowl acknowledged a playoff would do little to the game's fortunes.

"The Rose Bowl would survive," said Mitch Dorger, the game's CEO emeritus.

Take, then, the less-prestigious, not-nearly-as-rich Chick-fil-A Bowl. Once known as the Peach Bowl, it never had anything to do with crowning a national champion and regularly invites five-loss teams. It doesn't apologize for being anything more than a fun football game and cash cow.

Played New Year's Eve in Atlanta, it matches up one team from the ACC and one from the SEC, each usually within driving distance. It's a foolproof business plan, selling two big Southern fan bases on the idea of watching some football and partying in Buckhead. The game has sold out fourteen consecutive times, the second-longest streak behind the Rose Bowl. Facing little live sports competition, the game produced some the highest-rated bowl telecasts in ESPN history, and its 5.0 rating for South Carolina–Florida State in 2010 set a Chick-fil-A Bowl standard.

A playoff changes none of that. Even if the playoff plucks the best teams and forces bowls to dig deeper into the pool of eligible schools, the Chick-fil-A won't run out of middle-tier SEC teams. If it wasn't 7-5 Tennessee in 2009, it would've been 7-5 Georgia or 7-5 South Carolina.

As is the case for most games, four main revenue streams sustain the Chick-fil-A Bowl: ticket sales, a television contract, advertising/sponsorship, and a catchall that includes fundraising, merchandise, and government aid. For its game on New Year's Eve 2008, the Chick-fil-A pitted Clemson against Auburn. It produced $12.3 million in revenue.

Tickets raised $4.3 million and sponsorship $2.6 million. ESPN paid $2.5 million to broadcast the game, and the fundraising and merchandising arm brought $2.3 million. Unlike many games, the Chick-fil-A Bowl received no direct public money. The rest of the money came mostly from interest on investments and assets.

Assuming there was a playoff, the ticket sales wouldn't change. ESPN wouldn't drop a ratings winner. Fundraising, a local endeavor, would stay the same. Even the possibility of sponsorship money drying up, which is debatable, wouldn't threaten the game's existence.

Delany asserts a playoff would suck money away from bowl games. "It's a migratory dollar," he said. "And the dollar tends to follow those areas of those elements of a competitive season that are most attractive."

Never mind the incongruity of Delany admitting a playoff is more attractive than bowl games. The migratory dollar may not be so nomadic. Sports economist Andrew Zimbalist argues that as bigger corporate sponsors drive up prices on what would be higher-rated playoff games, other companies will simply seek more-affordable options. UDrove, an app for truckers, sponsored the Humanitarian Bowl, not the Fiesta Bowl, for a reason.

"As prices for sponsoring a playoff . . . rise, some corporations will return to the non-BCS bowls until the cost per thousand viewers (or some other metric) equalizes," Zimbalist wrote in his paper "The BCS, Antitrust, and Public Policy." "The proper output metric is not the number of games, but the number of fans consuming these games and the quantity of money spent in this consumption. There are very good reasons to believe that total bowl consumption and spending will increase under a playoff system."

More specifically to the Chick-fil-A Bowl, Zimbalist said in an interview that as with any bowl game, as long as television ratings are good, sponsors will follow. "There's not going to be any problem whatsoever," he said.

For the sake of this argument, we'll go with Delany's pessimistic prediction that the sponsorship money will go to the new, shiny, and infinitely more popular toy and never come back. That means $2.6 million, presumably the majority from Chick-fil-A, is at risk.

Worst-case scenario: The bowl retains 20 percent of its sponsorship, or about $500,000. Minor bowls such as the Liberty ($1.3 million) and Music City ($900,000) do better than that currently. Surely a sold-out, highly rated game will find enough local car dealers to churn up $500,000.

In that case, the Chick-fil-A would still produce $10.2 million in revenue. The bowl paid a combined $5.9 million to Auburn and Clemson in 2008. That leaves $4.3 million to stage a single football game. Since participating teams would continue to pay their own travel expenses and other costs, it leaves the true basics: Georgia Dome rent, paying referees, and other overhead. Such costs total about $1 million, according to bowl records.

That leaves $3.3 million for everything else: salaries, parties, travel for "scouting" weekends—really, whatever the leadership can dream up. The Chick-fil-A Bowl would manage. It spent $3.3 million in 2008 when flush with sponsorship money and lacking any incentive to watch expenses.

The 2008 Chick-fil-A Bowl turned a 16.9 percent profit. It couldn't waste its way to the break-even point, ending the year $2,073,747 in the black. Rather than give extra to the colleges that could use it or offer more to charity, the bowl put the profits into reserves. It ended the fiscal year with $15.7 million in total assets, including $8.1 million in cash.

This is an enterprise well capable of dealing with postseason competition and is primed to live as long as Methuselah. However much Cartel Kool-Aid Delany and Hancock consume, they cannot look at the Chick-fil-A Bowl and envision it disappearing.

"Of course bowl games are going to survive," Mountain West Conference commissioner Craig Thompson said. "If you understand the business, you know the bowls are not going to go away if a playoff is implemented."

Know this about the bowl system: It is not subject to a free market, and this is where the future of the smaller bowls comes into play. If left alone, the minor bowls would collapse, and they would collapse spectacularly.

The BCS operates much like a government, offering a form of welfare to ensure the survival of small bowls. Industry insiders estimate just fourteen of the thirty-five current bowl games are self-sufficient. The rest profit from a system that takes money from universities and guides it into the pockets of bowl operators.

An analysis of profit-and-loss statements for smaller bowl games (under $4 million in total revenue) showed that 35 to 40 percent of revenue comes from ticket guarantees. Title sponsorships for low-level games run as little as $250,000. Which means without athletic departments paying full price for empty seats, the bowl system collapses.

It's more shell game than bowl game. Take Minnesota, which agreed to buy 10,500 full-price tickets to the 2008 Insight Bowl in Tempe, Arizona, according to records the school filed with the NCAA. When Minnesota sold only 1,512, it incurred a $434,340 loss on tickets alone. It spent an additional $1.2 million on travel costs and other expenses. In the end, it cost Minnesota $1.7 million to collect the bowl's $1.2 million payout. In a vacuum, Minnesota's bowl experience would have been at least a half-million-dollar financial drain.

Power-conference teams are willing to lose money on smaller

bowls because their league peers cover the losses by participating in BCS games with $19.8 million payouts. The Big Ten pooled its bowl payout money and cut Minnesota a check that covered nearly all of its expenses.

Meanwhile, the Insight Bowl enjoyed its guaranteed ticket revenue. Despite close to 25,000 empty seats, it turned nearly a $1 million profit, according to tax records. In essence, the Rose Bowl funded the Insight Bowl. As long as the Big Ten agrees to an arrangement that cuts into its big-game profits, small games will go on forever. If the Insight Bowl operated in a real marketplace, Minnesota wouldn't play in a game that required it to pay its own way for nearly a week or buy full-price tickets it can't sell. In 2009, the bowl drew an anemic 0.4 television rating. Left to make an honest living, the Insight Bowl would likely wither and die.

This doesn't bother the Cartel. Actually, quite the opposite. For more than a decade, it has added games that couldn't stand on their own. Maybe it's because athletic directors receive bonuses for bowl appearances. Or because coaches use bowl appearances to fetch contract extensions. Or because conference commissioners push their salaries into the multimillions by citing, among other things, how many of their teams participated in a bowl. Or because none of the suits want to give up the freebies from the bowls.

"A few years ago, our ADs came to me and said, 'You've got to start some bowl games,'" Thompson said. "I said, 'You're going to lose money.' They said, 'I don't care.'"

Thompson obliged. Of the Mountain West's five bowl affiliates, one started in 2003, another in 2005, and one more in 2006. Before a three-year ban on new bowls was put in place in 2011, bowls were birthed nearly every year, all happy to be the newest Insight Bowl, a loser the system turns into a winner.

The Insight Bowl and others like it aren't alive because of tremendous business acumen. They exist because the Cartel says they should. It could pull the plug on 60 percent of the bowls tomorrow. Since it doesn't, these games—fundamentally flawed businesses—end up like factories with a government contract.

Most fans couldn't care less if a smaller bowl peters out. No one will write letters to Congress if the GoDaddy.com Bowl goes under. The Cartel nevertheless contends that the monetary losses, no matter how outrageous, are well worth it because they allow players, coaches, and athletic-department officials to have a "positive experience." Hancock, the BCS executive director and once head of the NCAA men's basketball tournament, said playing in a minor bowl game is a superior experience to March Madness. "It's an awesome thing," Hancock told radio host Dan Patrick.

If the Cartel believes money is immaterial and funding bowl games is a worthwhile expense, it guarantees that the bowls will never die. Especially not with a playoff, which would generate enough money to salvage the bowl system until the end of time.

Currently, the payouts for the thirty-five bowl games are worth about $275 million, nearly $175 million of which comes from the BCS. About $95 million of that is spent on travel, lodging, food, and unsold tickets. If the Cartel doesn't mind subsidizing bowl games to the tune of nearly nine figures when the gross revenue is $275 million, it isn't going to suddenly pull the plug when a playoff-plus-bowls generates around $1 billion. Governments don't cut the welfare rolls when tax revenue almost quadruples. Spending $95 million of $887.5 million in revenue is infinitely more palatable than $95 million of $275 million. If the Cartel has no problem allocating 34.5 percent to keep bottom-tier bowls now, it would be thrilled to pay just 10.7

percent. And, as an added bonus, trimming the fat from the bowl system lessens the likelihood of the biggest ones operating as such spendthrifts.

Either way, the dead bowls, universally accepted through the years as a consequence of a playoff, are merely a myth. As long as the BCS isn't inclined to commit bowl hara-kiri, the games will live long, fulfilled lives. Unless one of the Cartel's closest allies smartens up and goes turncoat.

Brains are the only real threat to bowl games. The system is safe until a conscientious president looks at the financial disaster that is the majority of bowls, starts asking questions, and sees what the bowl system hath wrought.

"The lower bowls are only susceptible because conferences might recognize that investment in bowls can no longer be justified," Western Athletic Conference commissioner Karl Benson said. "A playoff could allow more scrutiny and more assessment as to what is really a good business deal. So many bowls are bad business deals."

It would take a group of BCS-conference schools to realize they're paying for those bowl cocktail parties, an independent-thinking faction of presidents to take on the Cartel and proclaim it has twenty better places to spend $1.7 million than on some bowl with a 0.4 TV rating in Arizona.

That day could be approaching. *USA Today* reported in January 2010 that Division I-A athletic departments collectively needed $826 million in subsidies from taxpayers and student fees to balance their books. Just fourteen Division I-A athletic departments were in the black in fiscal 2009, according to an annual report from professor Daniel Fulks of Transylvania University, a liberal-arts school in Kentucky. The costs were real and considerable: Virginia hit up students for $11.9 million (6.2 percent of total student costs), and South Florida did the same for $12.5 million (8.3 percent). The median amount for campus support of athletics, from students, taxpayers, and other revenue not generated by the department, was $10.2 million at I-A schools, up 25.7 percent from 2008. The NCAA says colleges dropped 227 teams between 2007 and 2009, mostly due to budget shortfalls. The Knight Commission on Intercollegiate Athletics released a study in October 2009 that detailed the concerns of university presidents on those rising athletic costs. The report featured input from presidents representing 80 percent of Division I schools.

The commission concluded "university presidents at institutions with major football programs agree that current spending trends on intercollegiate athletics cannot be sustained nationally and collective action is needed to address escalating costs."

It is the impetus behind the expansion of the NCAA men's basketball tournament to sixty-eight teams as well as waves of conference realignments that have ended such historic rivalries as Oklahoma–Nebraska. The people who run college athletics will spit in the face of their traditions. They just won't mess with the Chick-fil-A Bowl.

The current system isn't coming close to meeting the financial needs of its athletic departments. If ever the presidents took collective action, the Welfare Bowls would make a prime target. Cutting out bottom-tier bowls would improve profits. The extra money could go to scholarships, improvements around campus, or even other sports instead of covering a trip for the football team to SeaWorld. Maintain the current system, and the risk that bowls die is far greater than if a playoff comes to save them.

It's painful to learn the abject shadiness of bowl games, from their backdoor deals to their outrageous executive salaries to their fudged payouts to their selfish priorities. Bowls, as a business, stink. And yet there's something innately good about them that muffles and ultimately mutes the shock: the football itself. Bowls are great because of the players and the coaches and the action and the excitement. The most compelling drama may be in the Rose Bowl one year and the Beef 'O' Brady's Bowl the next. The game doesn't discriminate. It always conquers. It deserves the best system possible, one whose weekdays teem with bowls and whose weekends sizzle with playoffs, a month-long cornucopia of college football madness.

Something that's positively alive.

9 It's Always Some Team Getting Screwed

In the weeks leading up to the 2005 national championship game, an e-mail chain circulated among a group of friends in the South. They were rabid Louisiana State football fans, the kind who write the word *go* with a Frenglish twist—*Geaux Tigers!*—and want to canonize Billy Cannon. They were angry. And they vowed revenge.

The ringleader was a man named Steve Cospolich. He was a twenty-six-year-old Internet consultant. He and his buddies scoffed at what they were hearing ad nauseam on ESPN: that USC, which would face Texas at the Rose Bowl in the BCS title game, was primed to win its third consecutive championship.

"They kept saying three-peat," Cospolich said, "and I wanted to know how you can have a three-peat if you don't even have two."

Just how many championships USC has won this millennium continues to be a matter of dispute. When it comes to the BCS, no one is ever really certain. It's not just small schools begging for access. It's not just unbeaten teams complaining about getting shafted. It's the actual BCS champion getting forgotten, and it happened to LSU in 2003.

At the end of that regular season, the Tigers were chosen to face Oklahoma in the BCS title game despite USC's superior ranking in the Associated Press and coaches' polls, both of which factored in the BCS formula. LSU and Oklahoma each had better computer ratings, even after the Sooners' embarrassing Big 12 Championship game loss to Kansas State, and that particular incarnation of the BCS formula failed to reward a dominant USC team whose sole defeat came in triple overtime at Cal. On January 4, 2004, LSU beat Oklahoma to win the BCS title. The Tigers were college football's official champion.

USC, meanwhile, romped over fourth-ranked Michigan. The writers voted the Trojans an overwhelming No. 1, and they received the unofficial title of people's champion. So impressive was USC that three coaches—obligated by contract to vote the BCS title-game winner No. 1—went rogue and chose the Trojans instead. President George W. Bush invited USC and LSU to the White House. The next year, USC went undefeated and was the undisputed champion, and it had run the table leading up to the 2006 championship game as well.

So when Texas upset USC 41–38 in the game of the decade, Cospolich and his friends hooted, hollered, and hatched their plan. There was no three-peat. In their minds, the Trojans didn't even have a repeat. One day after Texas's win, Cospolich and some friends launched a website called Onepeat.com. It was dead simple: a Photoshopped graphic poking fun at USC and, as a joke, a PayPal link next to it encouraging donations to fund a billboard in Los Angeles that needled Trojans fans. Cospolich figured he'd circulate it among LSU fans, catch a few laughs, and move on.

Something happened. One friend forwarded it to a few others. And those people passed it along to their buddies. And thus was born one of the biggest viral crazes to hit college football, one that resulted in a hundred thousand people dropping by Onepeat every day and giving that PayPal logo a serious workout.

Money poured in. Not just from Louisiana, either. A lawyer in Texas sent in $1,000. UCLA fans relished the chance to embarrass their nemesis. Even Notre Dame faithful supported Onepeat's cause. Cospolich did interviews on radio stations across the country. The New Orleans *Times-Picayune* splashed ONEPEAT across its front page. Within ten days, Cospolich had raised more than $10,000, and he had enough for his billboard campaign.

Five years later, looking back on his little contribution to college football history, Cospolich laughed. Onepeat was a success, no question, stirring the masses like any good BCS-related propaganda. It also reminded him of something that no LSU fan, nor the Cartel, really cares to acknowledge: Any national championship that needs ten grand and a billboard to legitimize it probably isn't worth a damn anyway.

"It's always some team getting screwed," Cospolich said.

For a system with one distinct mission—"It is nothing more than [an] attempt to match the No. 1 and No. 2 teams," according to the official BCS website—it is rather awful at its job. Of the thirteen national championship games since its inception, at least eight have provided questionable matchups.

Which is no surprise when the top two teams are determined by coaches who vote along political lines, Harris Poll electors with obvious regional biases, and computers whose influence is limited by the restrictions the BCS places on them. In 2005, USC thrashed Oklahoma 55–19 in the biggest blowout in BCS title-game history. Meanwhile, the coach of another undefeated major-conference team could only watch and wince.

"It still kills me," said Tommy Tuberville, coach of the Auburn team that finished 13-0 after a flawless eight-game SEC season. "I coached [as an assistant] in five national championship games at Miami. I knew what kind of team we had at Auburn. We beat five top 15 teams that year. USC and Oklahoma played three total between them. It's just so much politics."

Tuberville's beef resonates just like Cospolich's and the millions of other grudges against the BCS. LSU can't claim a national championship it owns. Perfection couldn't buy Auburn the chance to play for one. Tuberville rattles off the list of players from that '04 team: Cadillac Williams, Ronnie Brown, Jason Campbell, Marcus McNeill, Carlos Rogers, Jay Ratliff—"as good a team as we ever had at Miami," said Tuberville, now in his second year as head coach at Texas Tech.

No matter the talent, Tuberville recognized the near impossibility of a national championship game before the season even started. In the first polls of 2004, the AP and coaches' votes placed USC at No. 1 and Oklahoma at No. 2. Auburn was seventeenth with the writers, eighteenth with the coaches. Neither USC nor Oklahoma lost during the regular season, and no matter how impressive Tuberville's Tigers were—nor Utah, which finished the season unbeaten, too—the voters weren't going to endorse them over the Trojans or Sooners. Traditional powerhouses without a loss don't drop in the rankings. The computers agreed: None placed Auburn higher than third.

Auburn beat Virginia Tech in the Sugar Bowl, its consolation game, and Tuberville flew to Miami the next day to attend the Orange Bowl. Shortly before kickoff, he held a press conference to lobby voters to change their minds on Auburn. His populist appeal earned Auburn one first-place ballot in the AP poll despite USC's overwhelming win in the title game. The majority of voters listened, nodded along, and went back to the buffet, unmoved by Tuberville's speech that proved more prescient than convincing.

"This has created, and will continue to create, a lot of problems," he said that night, "when you have people determining a mythical national championship through polls and not having everyone play it out on the field. It's unfortunate that people won't get to see it played out like it should."

The wounds haven't healed in the years since. USC was later found guilty by the NCAA of major rules violations surrounding star running back Reggie Bush. One of the penalties was the vacating of the Orange Bowl victory over Oklahoma, which prompted the BCS to strip the Trojans of their title. It won't, however, retroactively award the title to Auburn. The Tigers were shut out by the BCS and will remain so.

It was far from the first BCS mess. The cluster at the top of the polls in 2000 foretold future chaos. Undefeated Oklahoma was the unquestioned No. 1 team. The BCS chose Florida State over Miami as the No. 2 team, even though the Hurricanes were ranked higher by the human polls and had beaten the Seminoles head-to-head during the season. Also in play was one-loss Washington, which had beaten Miami head-to-head only to be relegated to fourth mostly due to timing of its defeat. Miami cruised over Florida in the Sugar Bowl. Washington beat Purdue in the Rose Bowl. Florida State managed a safety against Oklahoma in a 13–2 championship-game loss that would've made a driver's-ed video look downright entertaining.

Even more egregious was 2001, when the BCS chose a team that didn't win its own division to play in the championship. Nebraska was undefeated through eleven games and inched its way to No. 2 in the polls before traveling to Colorado to lock up the Big 12 North title and a shot at the conference championship.

Over four embarrassing hours, Nebraska allowed 380 rushing yards, nearly 600 yards of total offense, and the most points in school history. Colorado kept running the same trap play, 98G, and the Nebraska defense regressed to Pop Warner level. Colorado running back Chris Brown scampered for six touchdowns, and that wasn't the worst part of the 62–36 loss. In everyone's mind—even Nebraska coach Frank Solich's—the national championship possibility was dead. The *Los Angeles Times* speculated that Nebraska would consider courting offers from the Cotton Bowl or Holiday Bowl.

Little did the Cornhuskers realize that a pair of upsets would vault them right back to where they were, second in the BCS standings, .05 point ahead of the Colorado team that smashed them, further proof that a loss is OK as long as . . . well, no one ever really figured out how a four-touchdown loss counted as a prerequisite for a national title–game appearance.

Oregon coach Mike Bellotti seethed. The Ducks, ranked second in both polls, were somehow fourth in the BCS standings, and they handily beat Colorado in the Fiesta Bowl. Bellotti had enough. He could no longer do the bidding of college football's powers that be and pretend like the BCS was a good idea. His evisceration of the system remains the angry standard for coaches.

"I liken the BCS to a bad disease, like cancer," Bellotti said. "Not to take anything away from Nebraska or Colorado—they're great football teams—but one has two losses and the other didn't win their conference championship. We're No. 2 in both polls, but those things don't have a lot of merit, obviously."

Very obviously, with the 2003 USC team that finished the regular season ranked No. 1 in both polls, a number that looked especially promising after Oklahoma lost by four touchdowns in its final game leading up to bowl season. Kansas State handed out the whipping this time, scoring 35 unanswered points on the Sooners, and still, the BCS divined that Oklahoma and LSU would make for a better game than USC and LSU. It led Trojans quarterback Matt Leinart to conduct a nationally televised interview while wearing a T-shirt that read "F*ck the BCS." An entrepreneur started selling them online within weeks. Cospolich wasn't the only one to take advantage of the BCS backlash.

"I think it stinks," then-USC coach Pete Carroll said. "I don't think it's the way it should be. But all we can do is keep talking about it."

And talk they have, from Tuberville asking for votes in 2004 to Les Miles using slick phraseology to back LSU into the 2007 BCS championship game over a plethora of other two-loss teams. The talk continued with another undefeated Utah team, in 2008, never getting its shot at a championship.

"We basically have a system for college football that too closely resembles the old Soviet Presidium," Air Force coach Troy Calhoun said. "You have a . . . politburo that's decided if you aren't one of those party members, then you're unable to participate."

Then came 2009, when five teams entered the bowl season undefeated, and 2010, when TCU capped its 13-0 season by beating Wisconsin in the Rose Bowl.

"There's really no true champion with the system that's in place," Utah coach Kyle Whittingham said.

"A change is imminent and necessary," Brigham Young coach Bronco Mendenhall said.

"You've got to blow it up and start over," Florida coach Urban Meyer once said, and remember that Meyer has won two BCS championships with the Gators. He also coached the 2004 Utah team that, along with USC and Auburn, finished the season undefeated. Meyer has lived the ultimate joy the BCS delivers, and he still sees its flaws.

"I was dead right," Tuberville said. "Sometimes I'll sit there and think, 'You will be the only team ever in the history of college football to go 13-0 in the SEC and not play for a championship.' I think we could've beaten USC. We'd played them hard the previous two years. We would have given them a game."

Just think: If Auburn had made the 2004 championship game, and if it had beaten USC, the college football world today would look mighty different. One of those changes would be in cyberspace, where Onepeat.com would be a domain name without an owner.

When the traffic died down and the donations stopped trickling in, the Onepeat gang counted the contributions: $11,625, more than enough to hang the billboard on 39th and Figueroa, next to the Los Angeles Memorial Coliseum and nearly kitty-corner from the USC campus. They had enough left over to order a car-hauled advertisement that drove around ESPN headquarters in Bristol, Connecticut, and reminded the network that its three-peat talk was nonsense.

Cospolich first worked out the finances. The L.A. billboard would cost about $5,000 and the mobile billboard around $4,000. They donated the remaining $2,625 to Hurricane Katrina victims, then went about the most important part of the plan: coming up with an effective slogan. Cospolich and his friends bandied about a few before settling on a simple, effective jab:

SHOULDN'T DYNASTIES
WIN MORE THAN ONE?

The billboard went up February 23, 2006, and LSU fans celebrated their victory. A self-professed "fat-cat alum" from USC named Kevin Robl promised to outdo Onepeat's billboard with one of his own in Baton Rouge. Locals threatened to vandalize it, and an LSU fan said he wanted to burn down Robl's house. No one ever saw a pro-USC billboard.

A little more than a week after the Los Angeles billboard poked across the L.A. skyline, Cospolich dispatched the mobile billboard to the ESPN campus for two days. As cathartic as this was, the bitterness remained. Cospolich's school won the national championship, and he needed to argue with people on behalf of its legitimacy.

"Every single statistical category that existed, we were better," said Shawn Mayeux, now Cospolich's business partner in the website Dealoco.com. "It's a subjective thing by the media. We lost to a ranked team. They lost to an unranked team in triple-overtime. It's all about what someone thinks. USC was a great team. I don't doubt that. Just because they whined about it doesn't mean they're national champions.

"It's college football. It's fun. But don't think that every time I hear the words *USC* and *national champions* I don't cringe."

Mayeux, Cospolich, and the rest of the Onepeat crew do take solace in their fortunes following the '04 championship. LSU won its second national championship in five years in 2007, and USC hasn't had a title since. Pete Carroll left two off-seasons ago for the NFL.

By the time LSU won its second BCS title, the Onepeat legend had permeated the purple-and-yellow crowd, and among the faithful, Cospolich was a hero, the guy everyone in the bar wanted to buy a drink. He fought for LSU and its crystal trophies, even if those titles were handed out by an organization that bastardizes the name of a championship.

"Whenever we go back to visit, there's always somebody who heard we were the Onepeat guys," Cospolich said. "And they love us."

10 Cowardice and Cupcakes

Former Michigan athletic director Bill Martin wanted something special for the opening game of the Wolverines' 2010 season. It would mark the unveiling of the renovated Michigan Stadium, a nearly quarter-billion-dollar facelift for the eighty-three-year-old Big House. Martin knew the historic date deserved a name opponent, not some weak Mid-American Conference team or, even worse, a nonentity out of Division I-AA.

He suspected some big-time schools would decline the opportunity. Still, Martin had a lot to offer. This was Michigan, after all, the winningest program in college football history. The game would be on national television. For recruiting purposes alone—the chance to play at one of the sport's great sanctuaries—it seemed a no-brainer.

Best of all, Martin was willing to do nearly anything, including return the game with a home date on the other school's campus. Michigan is the kind of opponent that drives ticket sales, excites alums, and draws high school prospects to town—the "Victors," the maize and blue, the winged helmet. This was Scheduling 101, Martin figured. Come to our place, we go to yours. Just about every school would jump at getting the iconic Wolverines for a home game, right?

Martin worked the phones, seeking any team from a major conference. Obviously, Florida, which hasn't played a regular-season, nonconference game outside of its home state since the BCS was created, wasn't going to sign on. Perhaps someone else from the SEC? Sorry. Maybe the Big 12? Or the then Pac-10? Texas and USC might say no, but a team from the middle of the pack? Hello? Anyone?

Martin felt like he was listening to a two-year-old: no, no, no, he kept hearing. The open date on his schedule stared at him, and he couldn't conceive mighty Michigan turning into some sort of a beggar. "I thought the allure of playing in the opening game of renovated Michigan Stadium would be a big draw," Martin said.

By July 2009, Martin was scrambling. The Wolverines needed an opponent, and the best they could find was a Big East program that hadn't played at the Division I-A level until 2000. Martin was thrilled nonetheless, because at least the University of Connecticut wanted to come to Ann Arbor and play in front of 110,000 people. Of course, that was as much for the 2013 return game at 40,000-seat Rentschler Field—the smallest venue to host the Wolverines in "as long as we can remember," Martin said—as anything.

"We got someone from a BCS conference," Martin said amid complaints from fans. "The fans have no idea how difficult that is to do. I'm excited we could do it. It was very, very difficult."

The Cartel will tell anyone within earshot that protecting the sanctity of the regular season is paramount and that a playoff would destroy it. Which is funny, because under the BCS the regular season has turned into a sham. Teams are rewarded for scheduling cupcake opponents in a blatant effort to either go undefeated or secure the six wins needed to guarantee bowl eligibility. September is a relative bore, and the days of coaches challenging their teams, seeking out national games, or offering value to their season-ticket holders is on life support when Michigan—Michigan!—can't even get a good game to reopen the Big House.

Because the polls reward teams with impressive records more than ones with impressive résumés, it discourages scheduling an early-season, out-of-conference challenge. Voters have proven over decades that they gravitate toward glossy records, no matter the opponents. Almost always, a major-conference team going 12-0 with a weak schedule is considered better than an 11-1 team that went through a meat grinder. The shiny zero clouds the concept of quality wins. The Cartel knows this and endorses it. By not providing voting criteria or, even better, establishing an informed selection committee, the Cartel has, by inaction, created a system that continues to further drain the very regular season it claims is so vital to the game's health.

"They took strength of schedule [and] minimized it," Oklahoma coach Bob Stoops said on *The Tim Brando Show.* "So now you don't see as many people playing tough nonconference schedules anymore."

To compete for a spot in the BCS title game, the road map is simple: Own a brand name and don't lose in the regular season. Texas didn't in 2009, and the Longhorns won the human vote ahead of undefeated Cincinnati, TCU, and Boise State. Texas, jobbed by the BCS before, learned how to work the system perfectly.

"They don't penalize you for playing weaker teams," Martin said. "Would we love to play Texas? You bet we would. I'd schedule them right now. We would love to play the traditional schools. But that isn't how it works anymore."

Such apprehension is routine among top-tier schools. It extends to the mid-level programs that rejected Michigan. Even teams with no realistic shot at a BCS title have little incentive to schedule an opponent against which they may struggle.

Bowl games, the Cartel's partners in obstruction, now feature seventy schools, or nearly 60 percent of the 120-team Division I-A. Athletic directors and coaches, most of whom collect five- or six-figure bonuses for reaching a bowl game, make up schedule. Missing out on a bowl is employment suicide, an automatic public damning, proof that a football program, most athletic departments' breadwinner, can't even back its way into mediocrity.

So ADs and coaches schedule to survive. If a team can start the season with a 4-0 record penciled in thanks to weak opponents, it need go only 2-6 in conference play to qualify for a bowl. In the world of the BCS, that counts as success and merits a bonus. It's a low standard, something the Cartel embraces. Poll voters care about records, bowl operators care about selling their tickets, and nobody cares about the nonconference schedule.

Or better put: No guts, plenty of glory. According to research by ESPN.com's Pat Forde, there were fifteen games in 1988 between nonconference teams ranked in the preseason top 20. In 2010, there were five. A year earlier, just four. For the entire country. Over the whole season, which since had expanded from eleven to twelve games.

While the system encourages big-name teams to schedule cream-puff nonconference games, it also rewards teams such as Boise State, with its easier-to-navigate conference schedules. This has been an unintended consequence for the Cartel. Playing in the Western Athletic Conference and moving to the Mountain West in 2011, Boise's road to an undefeated season is far easier than if it played in the SEC or Big 12. It doesn't have to run the weekly gauntlet of mostly good to great opponents, dealing with the inevitable injuries, letdowns, and huge opposing stadiums. The Broncos' season can boil down to one or two big nonconference games.

The BCS was designed to snuff out Boise State. It hasn't, which leaves major conference schools—and their presidents, like Ohio State's E. Gordon Gee—griping about the Broncos' schedule. A playoff would end the problem, making Boise State earn a title-game bid like everyone else, which is how the school wants it.

Boise State, due to its growing reputation, runs into trouble scheduling out-of-conference powerhouses. Like Michigan, it's on a constant search for quality nonconference opponents, only to find unreturned calls. And so goes the cycle, with the small-conference giants bumping their heads on the ceiling while the big-conference teams get fat on their peers' reputations.

Consider the 2007 Kansas Jayhawks, a team coming off a 6-6 season that, by the program's standards, wasn't half bad. They started the year with the following four nonconference opponents: Central Michigan, Florida International, Southeastern Louisiana, and Toledo, all at home. The Jayhawks rolled by a combined score of 214–23.

The queue of patsies—or, in this case, pastries—was so blatant that the *Lawrence Journal-World*'s website accompanied a story on the easy schedule with a picture of corpulent former coach Mark Mangino and the headline: "MANGINO: CUPCAKES SERVED THEIR PURPOSE."

The voters weren't laughing. They were too busy pushing the Jayhawks up the rankings. Due to a fortunate Big 12 schedule, Kansas didn't play Oklahoma, Texas, or Texas Tech that season. As they cruised through the season, the Jayhawks got to 11-0 without playing a single ranked team. Actually, forget ranked. They hardly played a winning team. Kansas beat just two Big 12 teams with records above .500: Texas A&M and Oklahoma State, both of which finished 7-6.

Yet prior to kickoff against Missouri in their regular-season finale, the Jayhawks were ranked No. 2 in the BCS standings. They had a clear path to the BCS title game. In a season where clearly superior teams had lost one game, Kansas parlayed its fortunate schedule into an unbeaten record, and beating lousy teams amounted to worthiness. These cupcakes were actually good for you.

Kansas wound up losing to Missouri and fell out of contention for the national championship. The Jayhawks did get a berth in the Orange Bowl—ahead of the Tigers, in fact—and acquitted themselves in victory. The point still resonated. Kansas almost rode a limp schedule into a shot for the title. Others copied the plan. Pride left college football's regular season long ago.

It was once taboo to play a Division I-AA opponent. Today they are sacrificial lambs, small schools happy to take a beatdown from a Division I-A school in exchange for a six-figure payday. Now only USC, UCLA, and Notre Dame resist sinking so low. Since 2005, games against I-AA opponents are up 70 percent nationally, according to *The Oregonian*. The once-proud Pac-12 has seen a 600 percent increase in I-AA games, and the Big Ten jumped 358 percent. One I-AA opponent is the new norm, and two isn't altogether frowned upon. If the voters and the bowl directors don't care, and the Cartel repeats its regular-season talking point often enough that people continue to believe it, schools will dive through loopholes.

One of every four nonconference SEC games comes against I-AA foes in 2011. The Big Ten plays 21 percent of its nonconference games against I-AA teams. Other conferences are just as guilty. Fans still pay full price to watch the slaughter, of course.

In 2008, Texas Tech gladly scheduled a pair of I-AA opponents, started 10-0, and stayed in the chase for a BCS title bid deep into November. Voters didn't care that its nonconference slate featured Eastern Washington and Massachusetts. Being unbeaten convinced the polls that the Red Raiders were the country's fifth-best team before they had faced another ranked team.

Former Texas Tech coach Mike Leach, a Pepperdine law school graduate and one of the smartest coaches in America, essentially shortened the season to eight games with his I-AA opponents, plus Nevada and Southern Methodist. He had to know it didn't matter whom he played in the nonconference season. *Sports Illustrated* reported Tech turned down overtures from LSU and played Eastern Washington instead. For the 2011 season, Texas Tech dumped a game with TCU only to keep one with Texas State.

Certainly the 2008 Red Raiders and 2007 Jayhawks were legitimate, capable of posting similar records against quality teams. They simply chose not to, taking the expressway over the craggy terrain. The BCS doesn't delineate between cowardice and strategy. If finishing unbeaten is the goal, teams might as well avoid trying to do it against twelve or thirteen major-conference opponents when eight will do. If every week is a playoff—as the Cartel wants the public to believe—there is no easier way to win the tournament than to play a bunch of No. 16 seeds.

Former USC coach Pete Carroll saw scheduling in a different, refreshing way. He ran his program based on the idea of competition. He challenged his players in practice and tried to translate that to Saturdays. Carroll craved the chance to test his team in hostile environments against some of the nation's storied programs. In a move almost unheard of anymore, he scheduled home-and-home series—one game at USC's stadium, one at the opponent's—against major-conference teams and opponents of note: Ohio State, Auburn, Notre Dame, Nebraska, Colorado, Arkansas, and Kansas State, among others.

Under Carroll, the Trojans filled their pre-Pac-10 schedule with quality teams. According to *Sports Illustrated*'s Stewart Mandel, 73 percent of the Trojans' nonconference games came against BCS conference teams. The national average is 36 percent and dropping. The Trojans should have been lauded and rewarded by the polls for doing what no other program does.

Instead, they found themselves punished for their schedule. Following its 2005 title-game loss, USC dropped games the next three seasons to huge underdogs. The stigma of Pac-10 letdowns followed the Trojans and buried them in the polls. Rather than take practical off weeks or shorten their schedule to nine Pac-10 games or cozy into the L.A. Coliseum for the year, the Trojans faced a major-conference opponent every week. They dodged more bullets. They dealt with more injuries. They brought the allure absent everywhere else in September. Yet they never got credit for the twelve-week grind no one else dared to try.

Florida entered the 2009 season as the consensus No. 1 team, coming off its second BCS title in three seasons with a loaded roster. The Gators scheduled Charleston Southern, Troy, and Florida International, along with their traditional game against Florida State. Texas, a preseason top 5 team, set up games with Louisiana-Monroe, Wyoming, Texas-El Paso, and Central Florida. Ole Miss, an upstart contender, followed Texas Tech's lead and went with two I-AA directional schools (Northern Arizona and Southeastern Louisiana) to accompany Alabama-Birmingham and Memphis. Penn State played home games against Akron, Syracuse, Temple, and Eastern Illinois.

This cries out for a solution. Saving the regular season, and protecting it from scheming ADs and coaches, demands a playoff with at-large selections to guarantee that a loss wouldn't torpedo any team's season. Big-conference teams wouldn't fear a nonconference challenge, as a defeat wouldn't slay their championship chances. Mid-tier teams would value victories against bigger, badder opponents, knowing it would boost their chances for an at-large bid. A selection committee told to weigh quality over quantity would reward the courageous, particularly when considering seeds.

Teams would line up to play a home-and-home with Michigan.

Instead, the Wolverines get UConn and we get the BCS playing the regular season's white knight when it's really the angel of death. All the bloviating comes from the same Cartel that knowingly deadens the schedule and makes it so that a game at the Big House is considered a nonstarter.

"I'm concerned, because I just don't see the strength-of-schedule philosophy being shared by as many people as we would hope if we're really concerned with the health of college football," Oklahoma athletic director Joe Castiglione, one of the nation's most aggressive schedulers, told ESPN.com. "There are some things on the horizon that make some of us wonder if it's a disincentive to scheduling harder nonconference games."

That's not protecting the sanctity of the regular season. That's ruining it.

Here's how the 2006–10 seasons should have ended . . .

2006 Bracket

1. Ohio State
(12-0) Big Ten champion

16. Troy
(7-5) Sun Belt champion

8. Oklahoma
(11-2) Big 12 champion

9. Boise State
(12-0) WAC champion

5. Wisconsin
(11-1) At-large bid

12. Wake Forest
(10-2) ACC champion

4. LSU
(10-2) At-large bid

13. BYU
(10-2) MWC champion

2. Florida
(12-1) SEC champion

15. Houston
(10-3) C-USA champion

7. USC
(10-2) Pac-10 champion

10. Auburn
(10-2) At-large bid

6. Louisville
(11-1) Big East champion

11. Notre Dame
(10-2) At-large bid

3. Michigan
(11-1) At-large bid

14. Central Michigan
(9-4) MAC champion

2007 Bracket

1. Ohio State
(11-1) Big Ten champion

16. Florida Atlantic
(7-5) Sun Belt champion

8. Kansas
(11-1) At-large bid

9. Hawaii
(12-0) WAC champion

5. Virginia Tech
(11-2) ACC champion

12. Arizona State
(10-2) At-large bid

4. Oklahoma
(11-2) Big 12 champion

13. BYU
(10-2) MWC champion

2. LSU
(11-2) SEC champion

15. Central Michigan
(8-5) MAC champion

7. Missouri
(11-2) At-large bid

10. West Virginia
(10-2) Big East champion

6. USC
(11-2) Pac-10 champion

11. Florida
(9-3) At-large bid

3. Georgia
(10-2) At-large bid

14. Central Florida
(10-3) C-USA champion

2008 Bracket

1. Oklahoma
(12-1) Big 12 champion

16. Buffalo
(8-5) MAC champion

8. Texas Tech
(11-1) At-large bid

9. Boise State
(12-0) WAC champion

5. USC
(11-1) Pac-10 champion

12. Cincinnati
(11-2) Big East champion

4. Alabama
(12-1) At-large bid

13. Virginia Tech
(9-4) ACC champion

2. Florida
(12-1) SEC champion

15. Troy
(8-4) Sun Belt champion

7. Penn State
(11-1) Big Ten champion

10. TCU
(10-2) At-large bid

6. Utah
(12-0) MWC champion

11. Ohio State
(10-2) At-large bid

3. Texas
(11-1) At-large bid

14. East Carolina
(9-4) C-USA champion

2009 Bracket

1. Alabama
(13-0) SEC champion

16. Troy
(9-3) Sun Belt champion

8. Ohio State
(10-2) Big Ten champion

9. Georgia Tech
(11-2) ACC champion

5. Florida
(12-1) At-large bid

12. Penn State
(10-2) At-large bid

4. TCU
(12-0) MWC champion

13. LSU
(9-3) At-large bid

2. Texas
(13-0) Big 12 champion

15. East Carolina
(9-4) C-USA champion

7. Oregon
(10-2) Pac-10 champion

10. Iowa
(10-2) At-large bid

6. Boise State
(13-0) WAC champion

11. Virginia Tech
(9-3) At-large bid

3. Cincinnati
(12-0) Big East champion

14. Central Michigan
(11-2) MAC champion

2010 Bracket

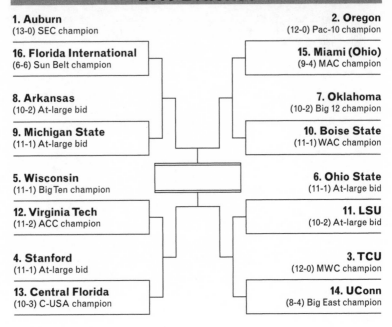

1. Auburn
(13-0) SEC champion

16. Florida International
(6-6) Sun Belt champion

8. Arkansas
(10-2) At-large bid

9. Michigan State
(11-1) At-large bid

5. Wisconsin
(11-1) Big Ten champion

12. Virginia Tech
(11-2) ACC champion

4. Stanford
(11-1) At-large bid

13. Central Florida
(10-3) C-USA champion

2. Oregon
(12-0) Pac-10 champion

15. Miami (Ohio)
(9-4) MAC champion

7. Oklahoma
(10-2) Big 12 champion

10. Boise State
(11-1) WAC champion

6. Ohio State
(11-1) At-large bid

11. LSU
(10-2) At-large bid

3. TCU
(12-0) MWC champion

14. UConn
(8-4) Big East champion

11 Diluting the Regular Season

In the final weeks of the 2009 NFL season, the Indianapolis Colts eschewed the pursuit of a perfect record to protect the health of their best players. They had clinched home-field advantage in the playoffs and didn't want a freak injury to torpedo their Super Bowl chances. So in late December against the New York Jets, quarterback Peyton Manning and others left in the third quarter with a lead and sat on the bench as the Colts blew the game and their unblemished season. A firestorm brewed soon thereafter, with Colts president Bill Polian and coach Jim Caldwell deemed pariahs for treating a potential 19-0 season as inconsequential. Fans across the country were merciless in their assessment: This was an awful way to end a season.

Of course, the Cartel was thrilled by the Colts' decision to tank. Off went a lightbulb in its collective head, albeit one that shone with the false glow of ignorance. Somehow, it came up with this argument against a playoff: If a team like Indianapolis is throwing games, how long until Ohio State just gives up against Michigan because its spot in the college tournament is set?

There are dozens of reasons this would never happen in college football. The Cartel chose to exploit the Colts anyway, never allowing the truth to get in the way. Reality is borne out by history: Never has a scenario arisen in which it would make mathematical sense for a team to sandbag games if there were a playoff. And it never will. Ever.

Not that the Cartel would allow such fly-by-night disciplines as math or history to stop its scare tactics. The Colts' argument, fallacious though it may be, became a centerpiece to the talking point that a playoff would irreparably harm the sport's regular season. Never mind that the weekly drama leading up to a sixteen-team, fifteen-game college football bonanza would be palpable—the number of critical games would multiply, and schools big and small would benefit. More games would matter, and they would matter more.

Anyone with a simple understanding of probability knows that Indianapolis' decision doesn't have any relation to what could or would happen in college football. That didn't stop BCS executive director Bill Hancock from sending out lengthy press releases and blog posts arguing the exact opposite.

"[The Colts' decision] does offer a real-life illustration of what an NFL-style playoff could do to college football's regular season," Hancock wrote.

Here's a real real-life illustration: The Colts compete with fifteen teams for the No. 1 seed in the AFC. Each team plays sixteen games, and barring a tie, overall record is the sole seeding criteria. In a college football playoff, 120 teams would vie for the No. 1 seed. Their bodies of work are twelve or thirteen games. The seeds would be based on myriad factors: record, strength of schedule, quality of victory, and how and when a team lost.

Only one scenario exists in which a college team would consider throwing its final game under a playoff system: If a team enters the final week of the season undefeated, and if every other team in college football has at least two losses, the undefeated team could conceivably lose its final game and keep the top seed. While records are a bit spotty dating all the way back to the first Princeton–Rutgers game in 1869, this potential scenario doesn't appear to have occurred at any time in college football's 132-year history.

In the NFL, where the thirty-two franchises' schedules are similar, teams often jump to a two-game advantage in the standings because they play sixteen times and compete for division titles with three teams. A college football team would need to take a two-game lead over 119 others, and do so while playing 20 to 25 percent fewer games. It's essentially impossible.

And even if somehow a team defied all known principles of applied math, it would need a coach willing to insult his players, anger his alumni, and butcher his recruiting while hoping the selection committee wouldn't ding the team for a late-season loss.

In reality, the chances for sandbagging are far greater under the current system. Because of the small number of teams competing for conference and division titles, the disproportionately large number of league games, and record being the only factor in determining league supremacy, it's common for teams to clinch either a league title or a berth in their conference title game with one or two regular-season appearances to spare.

Teams that lost early in the season and have no hopes of making the BCS title game have reached their pinnacle: either a BCS bowl bid or a shot at the conference championship game that gives them a chance at a BCS bowl. Technically, nothing prevents them from resting their starters in the final week. It could mean the difference between the Fiesta Bowl and the Insight Bowl.

Consider Ohio State in 2009. By mid-November, the Buckeyes had wrapped up the Big Ten title and a guaranteed a bid to the Rose Bowl. With two losses, however, they had no shot at the BCS championship leading into their game against archrival Michigan. By Hancock's reasoning, the game was meaning-less, a sandbag special. The Buckeyes went all out, of course, because rivalries are rivalries. They weren't the only ones. Geor-gia Tech and Central Michigan had no bowl-based incentive to win their regular-season finales, either, and could have rested starters to prepare for their conference title games. Nei-ther team did.

Under the BCS, Hancock's supposed "real-life illustration" of opportunities to tank not only were possible but happened three times in 2009 alone.

Under a playoff, its likelihood drops to infinitesimal. A playoff doesn't create the problem; it actually eliminates it.

Perhaps Hancock should move onto more likely calamities, like what to do if a blizzard hits the Orange Bowl.

The regular season is a bellwether issue for the Cartel, and so when one of its arguments rings hollow, it goes to its bag of half-truths and misdirection for another. None is more classic than making the BCS look prudent next to other sports.

Big Ten commissioner Jim Delany, for example, insinuates that men's college basketball—the NCAA's second most-popular sport—is a mess before March Madness, and a playoff would be just as ruinous for college football. "You look at college basket-ball, and I would say there's probably one must-see game during the regular season, Duke–North Carolina," he told *USA Today*.

While Michigan State basketball coach Tom Izzo and his Ohio State counterpart, Thad Matta, must appreciate their com-missioner disparaging their programs, the greater point is this: One of the most powerful men in college athletics compared two sports that are wildly dissimilar.

The men's basketball tournament boasts a field of sixty-eight, making entry fairly easy for major schools. The six big conferences have seventy-three teams playing basketball. Between their own automatic bids and thirty-seven at-large spots, they compete for forty-three available slots in the NCAA tournament. The rest go to champions of smaller conferences. That means 58.9 percent of major programs can potentially make the field. In 2011, for example, 49.3 percent (thirty-six teams) qualified.

Those same six conferences have sixty-seven football teams, including major independents Notre Dame and BYU. A maximum of eleven teams (16.4 percent) could make a playoff. Football's regular season would be a survival of the fittest, while basketball's amounts to a survival of the slightly out of shape.

Basketball teams play between thirty and thirty-five pre– NCAA tournament games, nearly three times the size of a football schedule, automatically diminishing any single result. Teams play as many as four times a week, which weakens the buildup to any one game. Archrivals face each other two or three times a year, not once, like in football. Conference tournaments allow a last-chance shot at an automatic bid even for cellar dwellers. And for the teams that do succeed in the regular season, the tournament rewards high seeds marginally: no home-court advantage and only a slightly easier tournament draw that, after the first round or two, is a wash.

"It is not an apt comparison," Texas athletic director DeLoss Dodds said, "because of the number of games." Football is apples. Basketball is oranges. Delany needs new taste buds.

The only similarity between college football and college basketball is that the players don't get paid. In the limited scope of some college administrators, this is apparently enough to base all assumptions on the future of one with the past of another. There are no other similarities. No one compares the relevancy of the regular season between the NBA and the NFL for plenty of reasons. The NBA stages an eighty-two-game regular season that diminishes the importance of any single game. It's far easier to qualify for the postseason in basketball: Sixteen of thirty teams (53.3 percent) make it. With four rounds of best-of-seven series, which can produce riveting action but take two months to complete, the NBA playoffs are a season unto themselves. And football is far more popular than basketball. ESPN produced record ratings for both pro leagues during the 2010 and 2011 seasons, yet the numbers aren't close. The NBA averaged a 1.6 Nielsen rating, the NFL a 10.5.

The NFL has none of the NBA's issues. Despite being saddled with a dreaded playoff system, its regular season remains a juggernaut of weekly viewership. NFL games accounted for the nineteen most-watched television shows of any kind, and twenty-eight of the top thirty during the fall of 2010, according to Nielsen. Only *Dancing with the Stars* prevented a clean thirty-for-thirty sweep. The NFL also produced the top fifteen shows on cable in 2010. NBC's *Sunday Night Football*, with an average of 21.4 million viewers, was the No. 1 show in all of television, a first for a sports program.

In a year when Americans seemingly couldn't get enough football, the college regular-season ratings managed to drop in 2010—CBS by 4.5 percent, ESPN2 10 percent, ABC 10.3 percent, and NBC 12.5 percent. ESPN was flat. Only Versus was up.

TV ratings aside, college football's regular season would remain more meaningful than the NFL's because there are 25 percent fewer games, one-off rivalry games, and a tougher path to the playoffs than the NFL, where 37.5 percent of teams make it.

"The regular season would retain its importance," said Neal Pilson, the former president of CBS Sports. "Teams are 2-8 and still playing for [rivalry games] and they draw full house and a strong television number. It's college football."

One of the Cartel's most oft-stated fears of even a plus-one playoff is "bracket creep," a term as ominous sounding as it is preposterous. The theory goes that if you start with four teams, the event will prove so popular and profitable that it will soon grow larger. Success, apparently, is a bad thing.

Hancock cites the ever-expanding NCAA men's basketball tournament as an example. This ignores the fact that the NFL hasn't expanded its playoffs for 21 years. Even with the 2011 work stoppage, it never considered doing so. If this were as much a legitimate worry as it is a canard, those in charge could sign a long-term media deal that locks in a four-team playoff for two decades. It's nothing more than an excuse to protect bowl executives who realize that while they may have a stake in a four-team playoff, once it goes past that, home sites would have to be used.

No matter how much the Cartel tries to win the regular-season argument, it can't, because its central premise—under the BCS, every week of the season is a playoff—amounts to nothing more than a marketing line.

Which regular-season game eliminated TCU in 2010 or Boise State, Cincinnati, and TCU from the 2009 playoff? None. Who knocked Utah out in 2008? Nobody. What sort of playoff leaves out an undefeated Auburn in 2004? Eliminating unbeaten teams doesn't fit most definitions of a playoff. Nor does a system that allows teams back in after they lose. In 2007, Illinois beat Ohio State in November. It was supposed to kill the Buckeyes' chance of playing in the BCS championship game. Two weeks later, LSU lost its regular-season finale to Arkansas. Gone, theoretically, were the Tigers' title hopes. The Cartel smiled. The every-week-is-a-playoff gambit looked smart.

Until January 7, that is, when the two teams that took the field at the Superdome in the BCS title game were Ohio State and LSU. Turns out every week is a playoff . . . except when it isn't.

A real playoff brings meaning back to September, adds excitement to October, and turns November into a footballpalooza where otherwise-obscure games draw widespread interest. Suddenly the MAC title game would be worth watching, because the winner becomes a first-round upset candidate. That's good for fans of the MAC and good for fans of college football. And, yeah, they're probably (Florida) Gator bait. Doesn't matter. The game will attract a crowd, the winning fans will storm the field like they won the national title, and they'll head to the biggest spectacle in college football instead of a lower-tier bowl.

Not just the smaller conferences benefit. The ACC title game, plagued by weak attendance, low ratings, and irrelevance under the BCS, would matter to everyone with a playoff. In 2009, fans of bubble teams would have tuned in to see whether Georgia Tech would win the league's automatic bid or lose and drop into the pool for one of the five at-large spots. When a real playoff plan is implemented, the implications of every game—from the ACC and Big East to the MAC and Mountain West—are far-reaching.

The chase for the five at-large bids would create a national free-for-all. The interlocking fortunes would take what people currently see as the thrill of college football and amplify it times ten. Any given Saturday in November currently provides four or five games with national implications. Imagine dozens of games, the fortunes of every bubble school shifting by the possession, a tapestry of drama. Scores would change, scenarios evolve, fortunes rise and fall, all too fast for ESPN's Rece Davis to dream up enough subtle one-liners.

"People would be watching to see who are the eight [playoff] teams going to be, or who are the sixteen [playoff] teams going to be," Dodds said. "It would build interest. It would enhance the season. You'd keep the TV interest [up] because now you're watching a game down in the Southeast to see the teams."

It's beautiful, this crescendo of college football, and all before the truest action begins in December. Instead of trying to embrace it, the Cartel comes up with every excuse possible, flimsiness no deterrent.

"You'd have a horrible argument over those [at-large bids]," former Pac-10 commissioner Tom Hansen told Dennis Dodd of CBSSports.com, and how rich that one of college football's great obstructionists talks about horrible arguments. The BCS is a Jenga tower of horrible arguments, each piece so easy to pick out, the foundation getting shakier and shakier. An educated selection committee would have some difficult decisions, sure, but it's silly to equate the fight over the sixty-eighth team in the men's basketball tournament with the final at-large bid in a football playoff. A better question: What's worse, fighting over which two-loss team to invite to the football playoff, or coming up with a way of explaining to an undefeated team why it wasn't worthy to compete for the national title?

By seeding the teams and offering home-field advantage to the best eight, the push to get to the top would create a secondary market of must-watch games.

The top 2 would have the right to host through the national semifinals. The top 3 teams would assume a traditionally easier first-round matchup against the Sun Belt, MAC, and Conference USA champions. The top 4 would get at least two home games and the top 8 one. Each step of the ladder is one more goal to pursue, one more race on which followers would fixate. While it seems impossible to make such games as Ohio State–Michigan, Auburn–Alabama, or Florida–Florida State more exciting, the fight for seeding would add that new dimension.

That's the thing about a playoff: It wouldn't just add opportunity or excitement to the postseason. It wouldn't simply crown a champion. It would reinvigorate the regular season, from the meaningful September to the exciting October to the wild November and on to the December and January that college football fans deserve.

12 Nonsense Math

Four years ago, a man named Hal Stern invited the nerds of the world to unite. Their enemy wasn't the typical scourge of jocks or acne but a faceless, inanimate entity that posed a threat to the credibility of all mathematicians.

Yes, the horror of the BCS extends beyond the sporting universe and into that of the bespectacled and pocket-protected. In an obscure math publication, the *Journal of Quantitative Analysis in Sports*, Stern wrote an impassioned plea to the men whose ranking systems compose the computerized portion of the formula that determines who plays in the BCS championship game: Don't allow the Cartel to corrupt you and the laws of mathematics.

"I am advocating a boycott of the Bowl Championship Series by all quantitative analysts," Stern wrote in his 2006 article, which has earned a cult following after the godfather of modern sports statistics, Bill James, jumped on the boycott bandwagon and urged his peers to do the same. Along for the ride are dozens of other analysts who make up an underground subculture fascinated with ranking college football teams in their spare time.

They wonder why the six chosen systems bother abiding by draconian BCS rules. The computer rankings, for example, are not allowed to take into consideration margin of victory. A 63–0 victory is the same as a 6–3 win. Jeff Sagarin, the most famous of the computer rankers, calls his BCS rankings the "politically correct" version and says they're "less accurate" than another version he calculates. It includes margin of victory, and the Cartel won't allow him to use it.

"You're asked to rank teams that don't play each other, that don't play long seasons, and you can't include margin of victory?" said Kenneth Massey, another of the handpicked mathematicians, who also provides a "better version" on his website. "It's a very challenging problem from a data-analysis standpoint. It does require sacrificing a bit of accuracy. It's not the best way to do it."

The entire point of the BCS using computerized ranking systems was to provide some sort of impartiality and to balance out the two human polls. The computers count for one-third of a team's BCS score. Of course, the first time they tried, the computers didn't jibe with the humans, so the Cartel changed the formula three years after the BCS started. Same for the second time the computers failed to agree with the voters. And the third. When the math didn't satisfy its standards—prop up the big schools, stomp on the small ones—the Cartel altered the formula.

"Stern's analysis was clearly right," said James, whose revolutionary work with baseball statistics was highlighted in the book *Moneyball* and who has since developed his own college football rating system. "This isn't a sincere effort to use math to find the answer at all. It's clearly an effort to use math as a cover for whatever you want to do. I don't even know if the people who set up the system are aware of that. It's just nonsense math."

The Cartel says it wants a fair and unbiased component. Instead, it's got another mess on its hands, one that turned into a talking point at the highest level of American politics. On

November 3, 2008, the night before the presidential election, Barack Obama appeared on *Monday Night Football*. He used the forum to reiterate a number of his positions. He also established a new one.

"I am fed up with these computer rankings," Obama said.

Obama's frustration was typical populist rhetoric. He didn't expound on why he disliked the computer rankings. He just disliked them. Truth is, the computers themselves aren't altogether terrible, and they're certainly not the overwhelming problem. The bigger issue is the system under which they operate, and how ignoring something so telling as margin of victory is far from the only blunder.

Take the actual computing itself. Every week, the six operators input scores, let the computers spit out the rankings, and send them to the BCS. That's it. Nobody at the BCS double-checks the rankings. Only one of the six, Wes Colley, makes his formula fully public. Which leaves five systems open for corruption with no safety net. Massey once admitted that if offered $1 million to doctor his standings, "It would take a lot of willpower to refuse that, to be sure." Rich boosters, forget that tailback recruit. Pool your money for this guy.

While no one is suggesting a payoff, Colley's rankings were twice found to be inaccurate in 2010 due to improper data entry. One came early in the season because the scoreboard source Colley uses—Rivals.com—wasn't up-to-date. The BCS didn't provide set data, and other programmers have found errors on the ESPN and CBS online scoreboards as well.

The second mistake came in the final rankings, when the result of a Division I-AA game between Appalachian State and Western Illinois wasn't entered. That minor result affected four teams in the top 20 and caused Boise State to leapfrog LSU for 10th in the final standings. The BCS had no idea until Jerry

Palm, who runs the independent CollegeBCS.com, discovered it by checking Colley's numbers. Only happenstance prevented a major controversy, as neither Boise nor LSU was in the title-game hunt. Hancock declared it "completely unacceptable," but the BCS seems happy to accept its mathematicians guarding their algorithms like they're the recipe for Coke. Even though the BCS has created a "peer review" method for the computer gurus to double-check each other's data, five of the six formulas remain secret. Hancock said in 2011 that the BCS had no plans on checking the results, which pits secrecy vs. accuracy for the foreseeable future. "I don't see an obvious resolution to the tension between those two concerns, and neither does anyone else," Colley said. As much scorn as Colley received for the mistake, he's the only one who could be caught because he's the only one willing to share his methodology. He should be applauded for the openness. The other five could be riddled with errors and no one, most notably the BCS, would have a clue.

"The BCS still doesn't have any idea what these guys are doing," Palm said. "This is my longstanding gripe with the system. No one is held accountable. There isn't any reason why they don't use open computer formulas except they either don't understand or they don't care."

The computer folks seem not to worry about the lack of transparency. Massey earned a Ph.D. at Virginia Tech and now teaches mathematics at Carson-Newman College. Sagarin is an MIT graduate who has ranked teams for *USA Today* since 1985. Colley is a bowtie-wearing, Princeton- and Harvard-educated astrophysicist who tries to solve everyday problems like traffic and freight delays. Another doctor, Peter Wolfe, specializes in infectious diseases when he's not obsessing over college football. Political scientist Jeff Anderson and freelance sportscaster Chris Hester started compiling rankings from Hester's mother's computer twenty years ago.

Then there is Richard Billingsley. He is sixty years old and lives in Hugo, Oklahoma. Unfailingly courteous, Billingsley speaks with a homespun voice that exudes calm. Though he's a stress-management expert by vocation, Billingsley follows his passion for college football in obsessive ways. Starting in 1970, he set out to name a national champion for every season dating back to 1869, when Princeton and Rutgers split the two games played. (Billingsley's verdict: Princeton.) His institutional history of college football is unquestioned. There's just one snag.

"I'm not a mathematician," Billingsley said.

A nonmathematician who uses a numbers-based formula to rank teams. A nonmathematician who, accordingly, employs the previous year's rankings as a starting point for the next year's, even if a school graduates its quarterback, running back, and middle linebacker, and loses its coach.

"I don't know that the powers that be even know what he's doing," Stern said. "I'm not saying he's bad. But . . . he's bad. It's clear it's not what the BCS should be doing."

Billingsley is unrepentant about using the previous season's results. He believes the past portends the future, even if the past is now playing in the NFL. The other computer systems that use preseason rankings take into account graduations, recruiting classes, and coaching changes—everything that matters.

"I'm not even a highly educated man, to tell you the truth," Billingsley said. "I don't even have a degree. I have a high school education. I never had calculus. I don't even remember much about algebra. I think everyone questions everything I do. Why is he doing that? Does he know what he's doing, a crazy kook in Oklahoma? I had a guy tell me in an e-mail once that I'm a crazy Oklahoma hillbilly. Well, it's true, but it has nothing to do with my ranking skills."

The actual skill involved is suspect. A Dutch computer scientist named Martien Maas, who has never been to a college football game but compiles rankings in his spare time, analyzed amateur ranking systems for their accuracy in picking bowl games in 2009. He assumed the success rate of predicting the correct winners would be somewhere between 75 and 85 percent. The computers barely chose 50 percent of the games correctly.

And yet the Cartel insists the computers are integral to the BCS system. They've been around longer than any other ranking systems, even the AP. Stern grew up in New York and looked forward to reading the *Long Island Press* so he could study the Dunkel Index, a ranking system that predated the first computer by a decade. The original power poll, devised by Illinois professor Frank Dickinson, started sometime in the mid-1920s and was followed by Dartmouth professor Dick Houlgate's in 1927. Dick Dunkel arrived in 1929, and today his grandsons Bob and Richard continue computing the Dunkel Index for college football, the NFL, and even the CFL and WNBA.

The acceptance of independent, numbers-based analysis took years. When David Rothman, whose progressive rankings influenced Sagarin, wrote NCAA executive director Walter Byers asking that his system be adopted by the organization, he received the following response: "Mr. Rothman, we will never do standings at the NCAA and second, we will never do yours."

Byers retired in 1988. Ten years later, when the BCS was born, the system centered on three computer rankings: Anderson and Hester, Sagarin, and the *New York Times*. The next year, the BCS added Billingsley, Massey, Rothman, the Dunkel Index, and Herman Matthews. In 2001, it dumped the *Times* and Dunkel rankings and replaced them with Wolfe and Colley. A year later, Rothman and Matthews were gone after refusing to remove margin of victory from their formulas.

Here's the reasoning behind the decision to banish margin

of victory before the 2002 season: The BCS didn't want teams that beat up on weaker opponents to be rewarded for doing so. Never mind that the BCS was actively corrupting the impartiality of its system. By mandating the removal of margin of victory, the BCS brought an issue patently tied to emotion—whether a blowout is right or wrong—into the machines it hired to be emotionless.

"Their action is crazy," Rothman told the *Cincinnati Enquirer*. "This makes the computer people look like hacks. It gives the impression of a lack of integrity."

To illustrate what he called "nonsense," Matthews removed margin of victory from the final rankings in which it was used, 2001, and sent the hypothetical results to the BCS. The starkest difference involved the University of Tennessee, which blew a chance at the national championship game by losing the SEC title to LSU and finished sixth in the BCS standings. It was Tennessee's second loss of the season, and yet without margin of victory, the Volunteers would have finished second in the BCS—ahead of one-loss teams from Nebraska and Oregon—and faced Miami in the championship game.

"That's really suspect," Matthews told the *Knoxville News Sentinel*. "Then Tennessee slaughtered Michigan [in the Citrus Bowl], but the Vols would have dropped from No. 2 to No. 3 while Michigan increased from No. 25 to No. 20. That's crazy."

Officially, the BCS's claims it did this in the name of sportsmanship, and nobody dislikes sportsmanship. Only the Cartel would argue that sportsmanship is a mathematical concept. The BCS neglected the numbers—the actual, objective data that a computer can measure—and the letters sent by Sagarin and Massey urging margin of victory's inclusion. It ignored the hypocrisy in letting the coaches and Harris Poll voters factor in margin of victory. It disregarded everyone who cares about the score of the game, which is pretty much anyone who watches. The computers were an easy scapegoat, and the BCS got rid of Rothman and Matthews because they refused to flout their mathematical principles.

Some of the computer rankers even parroted the illogical message.

"A significant but hard-to-measure factor in comparing teams is sportsmanship," Wolfe wrote on his website. "Running up the score is generally looked on as evidence of bad sportsmanship, behavior which should not be encouraged or rewarded."

The statistical community guffaws at Wolfe's concern with blowout victories while lamenting the BCS's decision. Any elementary mathematician, let alone someone with the ability to write a program that ranks every college football team, could figure out a way to limit margin of victory's effect—say, by making a thirty-point win count the same as a seventy-point win. In 2003, *American Statistician* devoted more than five thousand words to how removing margin of victory compromised the rankings. The magazine's research showed the two best algorithms were Rothman's and Matthews', both discarded by the BCS.

"It's about respecting and accepting what the math tells you," James said. "If it tells you Boise State is better than the teams that have the opportunity to play for the championship, what are you going to do?

"Well, if Boise State ever finishes first, they'll change [the formula] a fourth time."

James isn't exaggerating. The original version used computer rankings, human-poll rankings, a strength-of-schedule component, and number of losses. In 2001, the BCS added bonus points for quality wins. That wasn't good enough, so in 2002, it changed its quality-win formula and removed margin of victory. And after USC ended 2004 at No. 1 in the AP poll despite not playing for the BCS championship, the whole BCS system was blown up to deemphasize the computers.

Fall guys once, fall guys always.

Even the mathematicians warned the Cartel that the new system was untenable. "They looked at what we were trying to do and said . . . we're asking them to do an impossible job with imperfect tools," BCS consultant Kevin O'Malley told the Riverside (California) *Press-Enterprise*.

So, naturally, they went ahead with it anyway. The diluted computer rankings are determined rather simply. The six systems send in their twenty-five best teams, with the top one receiving 25 points and the lowest getting 1 point. For each team, the BCS drops the highest and lowest ranking to get rid of potential outliers, adds the four remaining numbers, divides them by one hundred to get a percentage, and averages that percentage with the ones from the coaches' poll and Harris Poll.

The computer guys do it because they love the challenge of competing against other minds, sort of like a science fair for adults. Otherwise, the fringe benefits are fringy. It's a good conversation starter. It's a license to brag when you get something correct, like Anderson and Hester did in 2008, when they ranked Utah second before its bowl victory against Alabama. None of the other computers had Utah higher than fourth. Even the Utes' coach, Kyle Whittingham, voted them fifth.

It's not for the money. The BCS pays only a nominal sum, not close to enough for the rankers to quit their jobs. And it's not for the swag. Colley, a longtime Alabama fan, wanted to attend the 2009 SEC championship game between Florida and the Crimson Tide. He figured a couple tickets wouldn't be much trouble.

"I e-mailed the SEC BCS liaison," Colley said, "and he just laughed at me."

To the rankers, the computer rankings are a chance to matter, and that's something they hold on to dearly. They see it as a privilege, no matter how corrupt the organization, how shady the leadership, how unpopular it is—or they are—among fans. The renown intoxicates them. The BCS chose them over more than a hundred others whose rankings appear on Massey's website, and it's good to feel important.

"We're part of history," Massey said, and he chewed on that idea for a moment, wondering whether it really is better to be a part of history that nobody supports than not to be part at all. He emerged from his quick philosophical debate with a compromise that seems downright shocking for someone employed by the BCS.

"I would like a playoff," Massey said.

He's not the only one.

"It's hard to argue with a sixteen-team playoff," Colley said.

Massey and Colley, and their ranking peers for that matter, are like so many others. They are good and smart people with noble intentions, and they work for bosses who make them look bad. The BCS is too strong a force. The nerds aren't ready for a revolution.

13 Fooling the Voters (Who Are Often Fools)

By the fourteenth year of their marriage, Kathy Miles understood what her husband, Les, needed after a devastating loss. She provided perspective amid his myopic self-loathing, the nurturing yin to his depressed yang. On this particular evening, one day after Thanksgiving in 2007, her attempt to comfort the Louisiana State football coach did more than work. With a little maternal optimism, Kathy Miles changed college football—and exposed another inherent flaw in the BCS.

LSU had blown a clear shot at the BCS title game by losing, in triple overtime, to Arkansas. This was the regular-season finale, and even though LSU was still headed to the SEC championship game, the Tigers' national championship hopes were bleak. Their record was 10-2, and later that weekend, LSU fell from No. 1 to No. 7 in the BCS rankings.

In the history of the BCS, no team with two losses had ever played for the championship. Miles feared he'd have to listen to another off-season about how Saint Nick Saban, LSU's previous coach, would have gone undefeated with all this talent. Kathy tried to divert Miles's mind by reminding him that the Tigers' other defeat came in triple OT, too.

"You know, Les," she said, "you're undefeated in regulation."

Miles's ears perked up. Undefeated in regulation. It was brilliant.

To coaches, a loss is a loss. There are no moral victories. Miles played for Bo Schembechler at Michigan, and nobody dared classify a defeat as a good one. But Miles knew the majority of people who determine the national championship aren't coaches, and that in the BCS, a loss is a loss only if the voters punish you for it.

If LSU wanted back into the national title picture, all Miles had to do was convince voters it deserved a spot there. And so began the ingenious campaign that would change the way BCS titles are won in college football: through the power of marketing brains as much as on-field brawn. The Tigers weren't trying to jockey the system and deny a small school its chance for glory. LSU would hopscotch its big-conference brethren with the first intensive spin-doctoring of the BCS era.

The morning after his wife offered up the best-sounding college football slogan since Notre Dame made Joe Theismann change the pronunciation of his name to rhyme with Heisman—and that one didn't work—Les Miles shared the line with a man named Michael Bonnette. He is LSU's sharp-mined associate athletic director in charge of media relations, and Bonnette would soon prove the importance of public relations personnel, a mostly overworked and underpaid lot that is now immensely influential.

"I was impressed by the simplicity of the argument," Bonnette said. "We had to argue to people, 'Yeah, we've got two losses, but look how they came.'"

LSU understood it had no control over the computer formulas, which compose one-third of the BCS formula that determines the title game. Miles and Bonnette targeted another weakness: the human polls, which make up the remaining two-thirds. The coaches' poll had sixty-one voters that year. The Harris Poll, a group of former college administrators, players, coaches, and media, had 114. And LSU was banking on the collective gullibility of those 173 men and two women to write its ticket to the championship game.

If the campaign gained traction and some other teams ahead of the Tigers in the BCS standings lost, they might slink back into the title-game discussion. It was a worthwhile Hail Mary, and Miles launched the plan during his weekly news conference.

"I like to talk about what we are and not what we lost," he said. "I look at a team that hasn't lost a game in regulation."

Plenty of eyes rolled. So did tape recorders, and reporters were more than happy to report Miles's assertion. He mentioned it again before the SEC title game in Atlanta, although his message was overshadowed by an erroneous report that he was about to become the head coach at Michigan. It was a nightmare for LSU, which wanted to stay on message.

LSU beat Tennessee that night, and the top 2 teams in the BCS standings, Missouri and West Virginia, lost. Miles immediately pounced, repeating his talking points. On the team's charter flight home, Bonnette worked the phones to key media and scored Miles a live interview on that night's *SportsCenter*. Back in Baton Rouge, Bonnette and his staff went to work on their propaganda. Bonnette believed the busy coaches and often-distracted Harris Poll voters wouldn't bother to digest more than a quick sound bite, if they even bothered to read their e-mails. And he suspected, quite accurately, that other schools had already drowned them in numbers with their appeals for title-game worthiness.

Instead, Bonnette put together a simple e-mail with four bullet points, the key being a central, emotional campaign slogan: "LSU is undefeated in regulation."

"We sold it," Bonnette said.

And the voters bought it in bulk. The Tigers, who had beaten fourteenth-ranked Tennessee in the SEC championship game, jumped to No. 2 in both polls, and the computers concurred, giving them a second-place finish in the BCS rankings and assuring them a berth in the national championship game. A month later, they handily beat Ohio State for the title.

Les Miles held the crystal trophy, and Kathy Miles cheered him on. Perhaps they should've switched places.

"I wish I could take credit for the line," Bonnette said.

While this wasn't the first major political push by a school, it indoctrinated the new era of unabashed, organized campaigns. Previously, teams relied on their conferences and broadcast partners to do their bidding. At halftime of the 2006 SEC championship game, with Florida ahead of Arkansas 17–7, SEC commissioner Mike Slive held a press conference and claimed that if the Gators won, they deserved the BCS title-game bid. "I'd be disappointed" if it didn't happen, he said. At the time, Slive was also serving as the BCS coordinator, which meant that the official head of the official postseason system officially admitted that he might not agree with the official result.

CBS turned the second half into an unpaid advertisement for the Gators. Color commentator Gary Danielson used on-air graphics and his telestrator to make points on behalf of the conference that approves of him before he broadcasts its games. Danielson later told Detroit sports radio station WXYT he did it only because he felt ESPN/ABC was going to do the same promotion for Michigan of the Big Ten, with whom the network has a broadcast contract.

In the press conference following Florida's 38–28 victory, its coach, Urban Meyer, not only pumped up the Gators but compared them to the Wolverines. Michigan coach Lloyd Carr, whose idle team entered the week ahead of Florida in the two polls but had lost its regular-season finale to Ohio State, called that "inappropriate." Perhaps, but it was effective. Florida surpassed Michigan in both polls and the BCS standings and went to Glendale, Arizona, and trounced Ohio State for the national title. Michigan watched, in part, because it wasn't as committed to the PR fight.

By 2008, sportswriters covering a November game between Oklahoma and Texas Tech watched their e-mail in-boxes fill up during the second half with missives from the University of Texas showing how a Sooners victory would affect the Longhorns' BCS fortunes. The preemptive attack was a brushstroke of the modern media game. Texas just didn't play it well enough. After OU handily won, Sooners coach Bob Stoops didn't dwell on the satisfying victory. He launched into a campaign spiel on why Oklahoma should get picked over the Longhorns, who earlier in the season had beaten the Sooners. OU went to its fourth championship game of the decade.

The in-house scheming increases by the season. Some schools have begun setting up mini–war rooms with interns monitoring the Web so they can counter arguments made on obscure blogs and fan message boards. The resources allocated to BCS politicking are approaching the levels devoted toward Heisman Trophy campaigns.

Coaches are uncomfortable with this new job requirement. Mack Brown of Texas said he longs for the days when a postgame press conference was about discussing a great victory, not trying to spin voters. "You can't just look at the end all the time," Brown said. "That's what the system is making everybody do. They're not enjoying the season."

Precious few coaches try to avoid the BCS clamor, and it's toughest for those like Boise State's Chris Petersen, whose Broncos finished the season undefeated three times and still weren't deemed worthy of the title game. Petersen refuses to politick—"It's never good enough," he said—and so the school and the Western Athletic Conference decided to do it for him. In 2009, they hired a local public relations firm to make the case Boise State deserved a major bowl bid.

The BCS had created the sporting version of the Iowa primary. And like anything that deals with a popular vote, the populace can be mind-numbingly dumb.

In 2005, the Associated Press, which runs the oldest and most respected college football poll, finally acknowledged the ethical problems with participating and told the BCS it didn't want its rankings involved in the process anymore. The AP's reasoning was sound: Staging an athletic competition based on a vote is ridiculous. The AP poll was created as a promotional tool designed to foster arguments. It was harmless fun. The BCS was not.

That left only the venerable coaches' poll, which rarely includes votes by the actual coaches. Overloaded with game preparation, recruiting, and bailing players out of the local jail, head coaches lack the time to watch teams around the country. Some can't be bothered to cast their own ballots. Those duties often fall to administrative assistants or media relations directors.

"I don't know why we vote," South Carolina coach Steve Spurrier said. "I guess we vote because college football is still without a playoff system. I really believe most coaches do not know a whole lot about the other teams."

Some votes are downright embarrassing. Missouri coach Gary Pinkel ranked a 12-0 Utah team fifteenth in the country at the end of 2008. Miles, the LSU coach, placed unbeaten Cincinnati eighth in the final ballot of 2009. The biases, whether big versus small, hewing to a region, or staying true to a conference, are blatant.

"I watched some of the voting patterns," former Kansas coach Mark Mangino told the *Denver Post*. "I can see areas where guys weren't voting for teams they probably should have."

Before the 2009 season, coaches told the Cartel they would participate if their weekly votes were anonymous. As such, fans couldn't sniff out the side deals and alliances. A coach trying to secure a BCS championship game spot could move his team to No. 1 and leave competitors off the ballot. The BCS wouldn't allow it, and the coaches caved.

In the final 2009 poll, Cincinnati and Texas Christian were fighting for a long-shot chance to sneak into the top 2 of the BCS standings. Cincinnati coach Brian Kelly voted his team No. 1 and TCU No. 4. TCU coach Gary Patterson ranked his team second and Cincinnati sixth. Imagine what they would've done had the Cartel not insisted their ballots be public. A secret ballot would forever kill the coaches' poll, and without that, the Cartel loses one of its best tools of collusion.

Another was born in 2005, after the AP withdrew. The BCS wanted a second human poll to balance the coaches' obvious prejudice. The more culprits, the better. Such was the impetus for the Harris Interactive College Football Poll, better known as the Harris Poll, a smorgasbord of people whose collective ignorance toward the current landscape of college football makes their voting even more foul than the coaches'.

While the media, coaches, and even coaches' secretaries aren't particularly adept at ranking teams, college football is the undeniable focus of their lives. Not so with Harris Poll voters, who aren't chosen by Harris Interactive or from some huge pool of applicants. Conferences nominate voters, whose history of back scratching is evident. While many Harris Poll voters are former players or administrators, they have families and businesses and other interests. Understandably, they follow the game only so much. That their previous involvement in football gives them sufficient expertise is like arguing that a long-retired Honda mechanic could service a 2011 hybrid.

A few years ago, a *New York Times* reporter tracked down a Harris voter at a construction site. The interview began after the voter laid down his jackhammer. In the final 2008 poll, the only one that really matters, CBS announcer Don Criqui didn't even bother to send in his ballot. Among those Harris Poll voters who do turn in their rankings, fingerprints of favoritism appear everywhere. In 2009, Eric Mizell, a former Troy State player, gave his twenty-fifth-place vote to—guess who?—the same Troy team that had yielded 56 points in nonconference losses to Florida and Alabama. In a ballot that assisted Cincinnati, Mike McGee voted TCU eighth, behind two-loss teams from Ohio State, Penn State, and Oregon. McGee used to be Cincinnati's athletic director.

The bias is complemented by an ignorance that permeates the Harris Poll. In November 2008, *Daily Oklahoman* columnist Berry Tramel asked Pat Quinn, a retired Oklahoma State media relations director and Harris Poll voter, which team was on top of his ballot. The following exchange happened.

QUINN: Oh, I don't know. Doesn't really matter.

TRAMEL: Really?

QUINN: I think Alabama and Penn State will probably play for the national championship.

TRAMEL: You do?

QUINN: They're the only undefeated teams, aren't they?

TRAMEL: Uh, actually, Penn State had a loss.

QUINN: Oh, well. Those Big Ten teams have a lot of votes.

This is someone the Cartel thinks is uniquely qualified to help determine its title-game matchup.

The University of Utah actually did go undefeated in 2008 but was relegated to the Sugar Bowl because nearly every Harris Poll voter ranked the school between sixth and tenth. The groupthink is undeniable. Voters admit they consult other polls when filling out their ballot, and it makes completely baseless preseason predictions important—death by *Athlon*, if you will.

The Mountain West Conference didn't have a major broadcast partner to do its bidding like the SEC or Big Ten does, and Utah's gaudy record provided no traction. Perception overwhelmed reality. Had Utah gone undefeated in the Pac-10, it probably would've played for the title. Instead, it ran the table in a league that had gone 6-1 against the Pac-10. By winning a better conference without the cachet, Utah was punished by voters who weren't paying attention.

When Utah manhandled Alabama in the Sugar Bowl to cap its 13-0 season, the college football world buzzed about the Utes' size and speed and skill and how they would've presented a far greater challenge than Oklahoma to national champion Florida. The voters had whiffed on Utah, and it was fair to seek out a few Harris Poll members and ask whether they bothered to even watch the Utes before dismissing them as unworthy of competing for a national title.

"I did not see them play," Bobby Aillet said.

"I didn't see any live games," Lance McIlhenny said. "I just [saw] highlights."

"I don't recall if I saw them play specifically during the

regular season," David Housel said. "I don't remember a specific game."

How long did it take to find those three blind voters? Three calls.

Fans of the biggest schools realized Utah, at the very least, deserved consideration for the title game. If voters aren't going to bother watching a 12-0 school—which had gone 12-0 four years earlier, too—nobody can defend the Harris Poll's credibility.

By offering no guidelines to voters, the BCS claims its formula comes about organically. That's a cop-out. Not requiring the voters to adhere to certain standards allows the Cartel to throw up its hands and say it had nothing to do with the results, even though it's aware that the most uninformed voters will default to the biggest brand name with the most TV exposure.

It's how Texas was chosen overwhelmingly by the 2009 voters. Cincinnati went undefeated, and Jeff Sagarin, the dean of computer rankings, deemed its conference, the Big East, tougher than the Big 12. TCU and Boise State went undefeated, and while their strength of schedule wasn't top-notch, each had beaten a team better than the Longhorns' best foe, Nebraska. That's how the Cartel likes it: The chase for a championship is nothing more than a popularity contest.

Poll voters have changed the way the college football is played. Start with the falsehood that excluding margin of victory in computer formulas somehow promotes sportsmanship. That isn't remotely the case. Consider Wisconsin's 83–20 dismantling of Indiana on November 13, 2010, which included 45 second-half points by the Badgers. UW coach Bret Bielema insisted he wasn't running up the score—his second- and third-stringers were just playing great. Close inspection of the game backs that up, and for the sake of this argument, let's accept Bielema's word, because it isn't important. The way poll voters reacted to his team's performance proved not only that he should've been trying to score 83, Bielema should've gone for 100.

Wisconsin entered the game ranked No. 6 in the BCS standings and fifth in both the Harris and coaches polls. Indiana was a weak opponent, winless in the Big Ten. The game was in Madison. There was little the Badgers could do to impress. They were supposed to win easily, after all.

The stakes for Wisconsin were high. The Badgers weren't just trying to reach the top 2 of the BCS standings for a title-game spot. They were battling Ohio State and Michigan State for a trip to the Rose Bowl. In lieu of a three-way tie—which would come to fruition—the Big Ten sends the team rated highest in the BCS to Pasadena. The Buckeyes were ranked No. 7, breathing down UW's neck even though the Badgers owned a head-to-head victory. Ohio State was set to close the season with games against Penn State, at ranked Iowa, and against their always-hyped rival, Michigan. All three were to be broadcast nationally, allowing plenty of opportunity to win over voters. Wisconsin closed with lower-profile contests against Indiana, Michigan, and Northwestern.

The best option for Wisconsin, whether Bielema knew it or not, was creating a wow-factor result in a game that otherwise would've been ignored by national poll voters. The 83-point outburst against Indiana made national news. It garnered additional ESPN highlight time, prime Internet site placement, and newspaper column inches.

Poll voters predictably noticed. None of the four teams ranked ahead of Wisconsin stumbled that week. In fact, no team in the top 18 lost. If anything, Wisconsin normally would hope to maintain their ground after playing the Big Ten's weakling. Instead, for beating a lousy team at home as everyone expected them to, the Badgers gained 39 points in the Harris Poll and 13 in the coaches' poll. Dozens of voters saw the 83 points as a sign of strength and legitimacy. They rewarded Wisconsin. While it didn't cause UW to move up a slot in the polls, it broadened their lead over Ohio State. The Buckeyes bested Penn State 38–14 yet actually lost votes—almost assuredly some to the Badgers— dropping 16 points in the coaches' poll and 3 in the Harris. The blowout worked.

It was little surprise two weeks later that Wisconsin hung a 70–23 victory on Northwestern. Bielema again argued he wasn't running up the score, which is fine. Even if he did, few could blame him. He didn't create a computer system that refuses to tell the difference between a 45–20 victory and an 83–20 victory. He didn't empower voters who reward a trivial final score. He didn't pick people who are too lazy to investigate the circumstances of the fourth-quarter onslaught. Or ones simply incapable of conceptualizing that the relative strength of Wisconsin and Indiana's third-teamers has no bearing on anything. Bielema had a Rose Bowl on the line, so doing what's best for his players—not the opponents—made sense.

On the other end of the spectrum, and even more troubling, was the night that the Oklahoma Sooners quit because of the BCS. On October 23, 2010, Missouri led OU 36–27 with 2:24 remaining in Columbia. Oklahoma had the ball and at least some hope of a miracle comeback. Overcoming a 9-point deficit in 2:24 isn't likely, but this is sports, the domain of legendary out-of-thin-air victories. Touchdown, onside kick, field goal, win. Sooner Magic reincarnated. Facing 4th and 10 from deep in his own territory, Oklahoma coach Bob Stoops elected to punt, effectively conceding the game to Missouri.

What looked like a concession was actually Stoops playing pragmatist: He feared that if OU failed to make a first down, Missouri would punch in an easy score, pushing the margin of defeat to 16. A double-digit number, he argued, would look worse to poll voters who have shown they can't decipher garbage-time scores from real ones. Stoops invented a new BCS-inspired concept: running down the score.

"It's a long year. Who knows how poll people look at scores?" Stoops told the *Oklahoman* about his curious decision that both confused and enraged many Sooner fans.

Stoops was absolutely correct, of course. Though it may be a depressing reality, this was smart off-the-field strategy defeating emotional on-the-field strategy. He argued to the media that if the Sooners won the rest of their games and there weren't two unbeaten major-conference teams, he could note their only defeat was a single-digit road loss to a quality opponent. Voters, Stoops surmised, would go for it. He may have had a good case. The following week, OU was the second-highest-ranked one-loss team. Perhaps the biggest indictment of poll voters was this: Stoops felt compelled to insult the core values of football because he knew voters' incompetence would harm his team otherwise. Worst of all is that the ignorance of BCS voters runs through a coach's mind in the middle of a fourth quarter when his team still could win the game.

The way around this is to accept the Mountain West Conference's request for a men's-basketball-style selection committee that would consist of a dozen educated voters with set criteria to consider and debate. A small group could accurately determine when a team is running up the score or when margin of defeat got out of hand because of honest effort. A dozen uncompromised people with a clear objective beats 175 who can't seem to get out of their own way. Though the endgame seems obvious, the Cartel won't bend.

"The system is working well," BCS executive director Bill Hancock said.

Absolutely. Except for the bumbling Harris Poll, the bogus coaches' poll, and a corrupt computer system. Other than all three parts of the formula used to fulfill the BCS's sole purpose, it's just dandy.

14 The Players' Choice

A. J. Green played wide receiver at the University of Georgia for three years, established himself as the best at his position, and wound up the fourth overall pick in the 2011 NFL Draft. In return for his performance with the Bulldogs, Green received the standard compensation for a college athlete, unchanged since the advent of Division I in 1973: the athletic scholarship. It includes tuition, room and board, books, and meals. It is, for those interested in their education, a nice perk. It is not, by any stretch of the imagination, a deal that represented Green's fair-market value.

His foray into the netherworld of memorabilia provided a better accounting of his worth. Early in 2010, Green sold his 2009 Independence Bowl jersey to an agent for $1,000. The NCAA found this out and suspended Green for the first four games of the 2010 season. Never mind the occupation of the person who bought it. If Green offloaded the jersey to a fan in Los Angeles or a homemaker in Athens, the penalty would have remained the same and the sanctimony ever apparent: As bowls profit by the millions and athletic-department employees cash bonus checks from the game, the players off of whom they profit are systematically shut out of sharing the wealth.

Should they dare try to partake, the NCAA sounds its amateurism alarm and sends in the cleanup crew. Its investigators pored through bank records the twenty-year-old Green provided, labeled him a cheater, and left him having to vouch for his character time and again for the crime of cashing in something he owned. Green said the NFL teams that asked him about the jersey hullabaloo laughed at college athletics' inherent hypocrisy.

Calling it anything less would be slathering on an inch-thick layer of sugar. On the day the NCAA suspended Green, twenty-two variations of his No. 8 jersey were for sale on Georgia's website, according to Andy Staples of *Sports Illustrated*, some for as much as $150 a pop. If a player selling his actual jersey makes him a lawbreaker, what does that make the school that peddles replicas?

"They are selling all their stuff and they're making all that money and you get, like, a meal check," Green said. "It's unfair, but that's their job. They don't care. They don't care about the players or what the players think."

To hear BCS executive director Bill Hancock explain it, college football's powerbrokers don't only care about the players. They exist for them. Of all the cockamamie excuses Hancock trotted out defending the BCS throughout the 2010 season, the spin he unveiled during his January 2011 address to the Football Writers Association of America rang so disingenuous, so desperately cloying that even by NCAA standards it came off as bad. Not only would the Cartel use college athletes to get rich, it would shove them out front as a human shield for all the arrows fired.

"As the people responsible for life on campus," Hancock said, "it's the job of university presidents and commissioners to look out for the best interest of the student-athletes—and that means preserving the regular season and protecting America's bowl tradition and experience.

"At its heart," he continued, "the BCS is a group of schools collaboratively doing what is in the best interest of their students."

Like with the 2010–11 Ohio State Buckeyes. Five players were caught selling gifts, peddling personal memorabilia, and exchanging autographs for tattoos. Star quarterback Terrelle Pryor sold his Fiesta Bowl sportsmanship award, which brought even more humor to the most oxymoronic honor in college athletics. Like Green, Pryor wasn't allowed to sell his own possessions. The award fetched Pryor a few hundred dollars, what amounted to a reprimand from then-coach Jim Tressel—"Very disappointing," he said—and a five-game suspension from the NCAA.

The BCS wasn't so disappointed in Pryor and his similarly suspended teammates to forget the business interests of its bowl cronies. When news broke that Ohio State could be without its best players for its Sugar Bowl game against Arkansas—a move that would cripple television ratings, ticket sales, and general excitement—the Cartel rallied. Sugar Bowl CEO Paul Hoolahan told the *Columbus Dispatch* he immediately lobbied for a one-game reprieve, thus moving the mass suspensions to the 2011 regular season.

"I made the point that anything that could be done to preserve the integrity of this year's game, we would greatly appreciate it," Hoolahan said. "That appeal did not fall on deaf ears."

Some of those ears belonged to Big Ten commissioner Jim Delany, who used his stature to lobby the appropriate NCAA regulatory committee on behalf of making the Buckeyes players bowl eligible. It worked. The NCAA cited the "unique opportunity these events provide" to give Pryor and his teammates a second chance. The obscure Paragraph 16 of the NCAA's Student-Athlete Reinstatement Policies and Procedures allows suspended players to return, CBSSports.com's Dennis Dodd reported, "in very limited circumstances if the next contest is the NCAA championship."

To which anybody could reply: The NCAA doesn't recognize a college football championship. Nowhere does the rule mention bowl games. Arkansas coach Bobby Petrino was as puzzled as anyone: "I don't understand how they were eligible," he said. "I just don't. And I never will." Understand it or not, Ohio State regained its top quarterback, running back, and wide receiver and beat the Razorbacks 31–26. Pryor won the game's MVP award.

It was one thing to learn later that Tressel knew of the memorabilia sales for nine months and, in violation of NCAA rules and his own contract, failed to turn over information and tried to cover up the incident, a series of decisions that led to his resignation in May 2011. For the NCAA to so misapply a rule simply for the Sugar Bowl's financial benefit angered even some in the Ohio State fan base uncomfortable with the "integrity" of a bowl game trumping the "integrity" of Woody Hayes's program. Hoolahan brushed off such concerns.

"I appreciate and fully understand the Midwestern values and ethics behind that," he said, "but I'm probably thinking of this from a selfish perspective."

At least Hoolahan didn't try to say he was doing it for the players.

Throughout the 2010 season, whenever he was starving for a lifeline, Bill Hancock would claim BCS critics were "too focused on money" while the Cartel was all about "the interests of the student-athlete." Never mind the fact that it's been rather well-established to this point that money guides conference commissioners' and bowl directors' every decision. The bowls, Hancock insisted, are for the players. With more than ten thousand in Division I-A football, anyone can find one or two or ten to say pretty much anything. Even the most forward-thinking, playoff-oriented twenty-year-old loves a road trip, a bag of swag, and a game on national television.

Hancock took it to another level, though, by applying unscientific analysis to an unscientific poll as the scientific basis for the BCS. In August 2010, *ESPN the Magazine*'s college football preview issue included a survey—dubbed College Football Confidential—of 135 players. It was meant to be entertaining copy in the middle of a magazine. It wasn't conducted by a reputable polling service. It didn't word questions properly. It failed to educate the players on the myriad of background information needed. It allowed only black-and-white answers. It sampled a very small number of a very large group. Most important: It didn't portend to be a definitive piece of work. The survey included questions about the use of hostesses in the recruiting process, which team has the most annoying mascot, and an inquiry into undergarments. (Only one respondent said he wore a cup.) No editor could have predicted the BCS would twist such a poll into the backbone of its existence.

The Cartel jumped at the chance to misrepresent a poll—it sounded plenty legitimate with ESPN's name attached—in unchallenged interviews. It turned a survey that concluded "players want a playoff" into a press release and repeated talking points that players don't want a playoff. Somehow, it caught traction.

Nate Silver interprets polls for a living as the heralded statistician and psephologist whose FiveThirtyEight polling aggregation website has proven amazingly accurate at predicting political elections. In 2008, he nailed forty-nine of fifty states in the presidential race and all thirty-five Senate seats. In 2009,

Time declared Silver one of the World's 100 Most Influential People. In 2010, the *New York Times* started to license FiveThirty-Eight on its website.

And in 2011, shown the *ESPN the Magazine* survey, Silver first laughed at the narrative woven by the BCS, and then declared, "The whole poll is suspect."

A breakdown of the three questions that pertained to the postseason shows just how Cartel propaganda works.

Question No. 1: Do you want a playoff?

Yes: 62.2 percent

No: 37.8 percent

Seems pretty straightforward: Players favored a playoff by nearly a two-to-one margin. This was the only question in the survey with which Silver had no issues.

"Once you ask, 'Do you want a playoff or not?'" he said, "that seems like the necessary and sufficient question to address the issue."

Question No. 2: Would you rather have a [I-AA]-style, 16-team playoff [no bowls] or the current system?

[I-AA]: 29.6 percent

Current system: 70.4 percent

Polling 101: Never build a question around a false premise. "You have to ask questions that are thought of carefully," Silver said. And considering that a playoff of any size and the bowl system easily can coexist, it's at best a loaded question, at worst a misleading and misrepresenting one.

Seventy teams get to play in a bowl and only sixteen in the ESPN-proposed scenario, and if a player doubts his team's ability to crack the playoff bracket, the bowl wins out. Since selection criteria were never mentioned (is there automatic qualifying?), thousands of players might figure they'd never stand a chance at any postseason.

"I don't think guys would say they dislike a bowl game," said David Paulson, an All-Pac-10 tight end at Oregon. "But it's hard to compare it to a playoff system. Players don't really have experience with both. [The BCS] could say [bowl games exist] because we like it. But of course players are going to say they like it. They don't know what the alternative is."

The survey suggested as much. It cited "one SEC voter" who voted against the sixteen-team playoff, in part because he preferred a thirty-two-team event. "I'd like to see a playoff, but we're not going to get that without answering a lot of tough questions," the unnamed voter said. The BCS never seems to cite his answer in its press releases.

Hancock does enjoy comparing Division I-A and I-AA, a specious argument heavy with connotation. No bowl games exist at the I-AA level—which actually features a twenty-team playoff—because it lacks the requisite fans, television ratings, and loss-absorbing budgets to mimic the sort of business expected by bowls. If I-AA schools could, or were willing to, lose millions playing bowl games, you can bet someone would create such bowls and take their money.

"The logical thing to do if you want to have balance," Silver said, "is ask, 'What would you think about a sixteen-team playoff if we did have the bowl games?' You need to give an Option A, Option B, or Option C."

When offered a vision of what a playoff might look like— say, with games on campus—players' eyes light up. "That would be crazy, a great scene," said DeMarco Murray, Oklahoma's star running back in 2010–11. "We had the best fans, and to have that kind of excitement on campus, in Norman? It would be incredible, a lot of fun."

Alongside those games, the bowls could operate per usual as long as conferences subsidize them. The non-BCS bowls would continue as is, enjoyable made-for-TV events with no bearing on determining No. 1.

"Having a national championship is not going to make the GoDaddy.com Bowl any better or any worse," Oregon defensive end Nick Musgrove, a staunch playoff supporter even though he played in a BCS title game, told Fanhouse.com. "How relevant are the [minor] bowls now?"

Question No. 3: Would you rather have a college football career with three bowl trips or one playoff trip?

Three bowls: 77 percent

One playoff: 23 percent

Would you rather have three Olympics appearances or one medal? Maybe three tickets to a regular-season NFL game or one to the Super Bowl? How about three Oreos or one chocolate chip cookie? You could just as easily ask: Would you rather reach one BCS championship game or three regular bowls? It doesn't have anything to do with anything. Which probably explains why the BCS cited its results most often in media interviews. Hancock never mentioned the first question, where the players conclude they "want a playoff."

"One of the most basic litmus tests for whether someone is spinning or having an honest conversation is whether they cherry-pick one result from a poll rather than display a larger picture," Silver said. "When you have another question from a larger survey that is more germane and don't report that result and report a secondary question that is somewhat misleading, you have no intentions of actually presenting something honestly."

The National College Players Association, on the other hand, tries to advocate for the interests of players. In 1995, UCLA All-American linebacker Donnie Edwards served a one-game suspension for accepting less than $200 in groceries. It infuriated his backup, Ramogi Huma, enough that he dedicated himself to pushing the NCAA on issues such as player safety, improved health care, higher living expenses, and other problems long ignored by college sports leaders.

The NCPA ran its own poll in 2011 and found that "81 percent of respondents favor a playoff to determine the national champion. After reviewing various playoff models, the percentage of those in support of a playoff jumps to 89 percent." The most popular playoff system among players was the sixteen-team, eleven-conference championship model.

"Football players dedicate themselves year round for a fair opportunity to compete for a national championship," Huma said. "It is unsportsmanlike for conference and bowl commissioners to stack the odds against some schools in favor of others. We conducted this survey because the guys who actually play the sport should have some say."

Granted, the NCPA's poll contained some of the same flaws as *ESPN the Magazine*'s. While Huma sent the survey to one thousand people, he received only 185 responses, too small a sample size for any statistical significance. Selection bias existed. Even if it was better than ESPN's, with the depth and breadth of the questions, it still wasn't the sort of survey Gallup or Ipsos can produce. Surely the BCS could afford to commission one. A top-of-the-line poll, Silver said, would cost around $30,000.

In other words, less than a John Junker birthday party.

"I'm guessing they don't do that," Silver said, "because they know they won't like what they see."

Around two hundred years of experience and wisdom in college athletics resides inside the Cartel's innermost core. The members sit on important committees, draw up policy, and help guide the sport. The NCAA is run by these people, not the worker bees at the central office in Indianapolis. The conference commissioners can rewrite any and all parts of the NCAA rulebook or business model. They can do it virtually overnight. So if they're now suddenly interested in listening to the football players, well, the first thing they can do is start paying them.

Won't find any player polls against that.

They could also guarantee scholarships for five years, not the current one year that leaves players susceptible to performance, injuries, and coaching changes. They could eliminate the one-sided—and patently unfair—National Letter of Intent, which tethers an athlete to one school without guaranteeing a scholarship. They could begin providing lifelong health care for players who suffer catastrophic injuries. They could rewrite the mountainous rulebook that players struggle to navigate. They could eliminate over-signing, the practice where schools bring in more players than the scholarship limit allows and can result in athletes being bounced from school even after spending months in class.

They could guarantee that athletes can be released from scholarships if they wish to transfer and not be restricted on where they can go. They could eliminate the one-year ban from playing at their new school. They could cut practice time and demands from coaches to help foster not just higher graduation rates but actual education. They could stop forcing players to sign away the legal rights to their likeness in perpetuity so the NCAA can continue to profit off ex-players in television commercials, video games, and memorabilia sales, the core issue of a class-action lawsuit led by former UCLA basketball player Ed O'Bannon and Cincinnati star Oscar Robertson. "The arrogance and greed of the NCAA knows no bounds," said the Big O, who, fifty-one years after leaving campus, still watches college sports produce trading cards of him without permission or compensation.

They could provide complimentary travel for the players' families to the NCAA basketball tournament or major bowl games, where costs can be prohibitive. They could force bowl games to provide free tickets for parents. They could reform just about everything player polls would no doubt find troubling about college athletics. Yet their benevolence and bounties go instead to their golfing buddies who run the bowl system.

"Of course they use us," said Oregon's Paulson. "There are things we want that won't ever get put in place."

During his speech to the football writers, Bill Hancock couldn't stop talking about the kids, harping on the kids, extolling the bowls' virtues for the kids. For the first time ever, college sports was completely about the kids. He resembled a pitchman who had run out of ideas.

"I certainly understand the lure of filling out a bracket, kicking up your feet with a bag of Tostitos and a jar of queso, and enjoying the excitement of a four-week playoff from your sofa at home," Hancock said, making sure to slip in the name of a corporate sponsor. "But is that in the best interest of the students, whose voices too frequently get lost in this debate?"

"Settle it on the field," A. J. Green said.

"Settle it on the field," DeMarco Murray said.

"Settle it on the field," David Paulson said.

Those voices sound loud and clear. They're something the Cartel never has cared about. And never will.

15 The Superfan

As a reporter for *Buckeye Sports Bulletin*, a weekly newspaper dedicated to covering Ohio State sports, Steve Helwagen wrote stories about the football team year-round—features, tidbits, interviews, anything he could find, even in the dead of June. It was a niche publication, desperate to reach Ohio State's vast alumni network. In 1997, a year before the BCS was born, the *Bulletin* started posting stories on the Internet.

At the time, year-round media coverage of college football hardly existed. During the off-season, the local *Columbus Dispatch* would go weeks between reports on the Buckeyes. Unless something major happened, "there was nothing," Helwagen said. The sport was still rooted in its past as a seasonal pursuit. So when Helwagen told people what he did for a living, they usually looked at him sideways—even in football-mad Columbus.

Today, Helwagen is the managing editor of the online fan site Bucknuts.com, which draws up to 5 million page views and 200,000 unique users a month, more than 5,000 of whom pay $100 for a yearly subscription to get every last bit of news and gossip possible on their favorite team. Ohio State fever is a multimillion-dollar business. BuckeyeGrove.com, BuckeyeSports .com, and The-Ozone.net also take a piece of Ohio State's mega-audience, each site larded with minutiae and fan message boards that spin twenty-four hours a day, 365 days a year.

The Internet has bred a new sort of sports consumer: the Superfan, a plugged-in, often maniacal follower who devotes massive amounts of time and money to following a sport. College football claims millions of them. Superfans know more about the team and the sport than their ancestors ever could. They watch, read, interact, debate, and live it. They travel to more games, absorb every morsel of news, and obsess not simply over national signing day but over unofficial visits of high school sophomores.

Almost nothing is the same as it was before the Internet changed the game—except the system that governs college football's championship.

The Cartel congratulates itself for the spike in college football's popularity, which is the sporting equivalent of Al Gore taking credit for creating the Internet. The BCS wasn't an engine for college football's rise. It's an anchor with a broken reel. Thirteen years ago, the Cartel formed the BCS to avoid one of its most pertinent problems: split national titles, such as the one Nebraska and Michigan shared in 1997. It hasn't even managed to do that: LSU and USC were co-champions in 2003.

The BCS is woefully outdated, a dial-up connection in the high-speed-wireless era. Businesses today modernize by the minute or die, and the Cartel has approved one significant change since its inception: adding a fifth BCS game. Perhaps no other consumer-driven industry has changed less in these adapt-or-vanish times. And the Cartel wonders why fans holler with such vitriol when the BCS goes bad.

Superfans beg for evolution. They want a playoff for the additional excitement, for the season that roars to a conclusion instead of stalling out and hoping it got things right. They want to see who's best, without any maybes attached. The amount and depth of coverage has grown exponentially in the last five years. An avalanche of information and the ability for fans to engage with each other on message boards, in chat rooms, and through Twitter feeds have launched interest in the sport to stratospheric levels, placing college football behind only the NFL in popularity.

Even the dinosaurs of print media recognized the need to change. More than a half-dozen Ohio newspapers now staff the team from January 1 to December 31. They rarely miss a day, even in the off-season, to give Ohio State fans their football fix. They blog. They tweet. They chat. Joining them are the two full-time sports talk radio stations in Columbus that go heavy on the Buckeyes.

Forget an off-season. On the hyper-focused Internet, there's no longer an off-afternoon. And it's not just Ohio State. College football is a massive product with a ravenous audience and providers happy to oblige. No one questions what Helwagen does for a living anymore.

"Now they ask about recruits," he said. "For fans, it's a borderline obsession. People build their year around following college football."

Consider the once-humble spring game, which used to be an informal intrasquad scrimmage to offer players a light at the end of the off-season workout tunnel. Now it's a downright event, some televised locally and, thanks to ESPN, nationally. In 2007, 92,138 fans packed Bryant-Denny Stadium to witness Nick Saban's first Alabama spring game. *Sports Illustrated* featured it in a cover story. Not to be outdone, Ohio State set a new spring-practice attendance record in 2009 when 95,722 watched the Buckeyes in a practice game.

"When people make that kind of emotional and financial investment to being a fan of a particular college, they have an expectation that their school is going to be treated fairly," Helwagen said. "When it's not, that's a big problem."

Bigger than the Cartel realizes. The Superfan demands answers, the BCS offers excuses. The Cartel fiddles while the fans' anger burns.

In 2009, when the University of Cincinnati was en route to becoming just the second BCS conference team to go unbeaten and be shut out of the title game, the school's Superfans were enraged. They felt the system cheated their team, denied it an opportunity—said the Bearcats weren't worthy because their stadium was too small, or their team's history not illustrious enough, or some other dubious reason.

For decades, college fans were accustomed to unbeaten seasons sometimes not resulting in a No. 1 ranking. Now they can't tolerate such injustices. Joe Paterno had it happen to him four times at Penn State, including as recently as 1994. In 1968–69, Penn State had back-to-back 11-0 seasons and didn't win a title either time. Everyone shrugged and accepted the order of the bureaucracy, the limitations of the system. They complained in State College diners and bars. Fans today unload on the Internet.

To counter the Cincinnati uprising, executive director Bill Hancock appeared on Dan Patrick's syndicated radio show, where Hancock said that as a consolation prize he'd give then–Bearcats coach Brian Kelly a hearty pat on the back and tell him, "You guys had a great season and you're to be congratulated for it."

It wasn't just Cincinnati fan message boards that almost collapsed in anger. Superfans across the country were outraged at Hancock's condescending and patronizing answer. He was mocking their team and, by proxy, their commitment. The fight between fans and the BCS isn't just a matchup of slow-witted executives and angry customers. It's a clash of cultures and generations, and it's one the Cartel will never win.

Each year, another group of young fans demanding modernization of the sport is born while a group that still believes

in the value of backslaps and cherishes memories of the Blue-
bonnet Bowl fades away. The demographics will eventually
topple the system.

"There's nothing like the Internet, and there never has
been," said Bobby Burton, a former University of Texas football
manager and recruiting newsletter editor who created the
spawning ground of the Superfan when he purchased and re-
branded Rivals.com in 2001. The leader of the modern fan-site
industry was a late convert, not logging on to the Internet until
1997. That day at a friend's house, Burton experienced everything the Internet could be: addictive, fulfilling, and ripe for
the sports fan.

"I went on at about 10 P.M. and I probably didn't get off
until four in the morning," he said. "It kind of grabbed me immediately. I had no idea what it could turn into today, but I
knew as a medium it is unmatched in many ways."

Less than four years later he was part of a partnership group
that took over Rivals, then a bankrupt, post-Internet-bubble
company featuring a ragtag string of websites attached to fan
magazines—*Irish Illustrated* at Notre Dame, *Spartan* magazine
at Michigan State, *Tiger Illustrated* at Clemson. Knowing that
endless information and a place to discuss it would attract readers, Rivals started individual sites for every major Division I-A
school and encouraged them to focus on recruiting team news
big and small, and, of course, message boards that would grow
into massive communities. In 2007, Yahoo! bought the company
for a reported $90 million.

"In the early days, people tried to compare the Internet to
talk radio because they thought it was a bunch of mindless chat-
ter," Burton said. "But the reality is the power of the community is so much more than talk radio could be. Talk radio talks
at you. With the Internet, it's so much more about involve-

ment on a personal level. The appetite is there. We just fed the hungry."

Soon everyone was trying to satisfy an insatiable fan base. Recruiting, previously newsworthy only on signing day, became an industry. Independent sites like Bucknuts.com sprang up across the Web. Nearly every major-conference program has between two and four sites dedicated to it. Blogs—from the wry Every Day Should Be Saturday to MGoBlog that covers Michigan— offered coverage at a depth never before contemplated.

Sports talk radio exploded as a medium and moved from beyond the pro sports–dominated big cities to college towns. The Internet took low-watt, mom-and-pop stations and allowed them to stream around the globe. An expat in Istanbul could walk around Taksim Square listening to a podcast about Virginia Tech football on his iPhone and then pull up a browser and post his thoughts on a message board. No longer does it matter if you live in Blacksburg or by the Black Sea. Everything is available to readers who live in a campus dormitory or half a world away.

During the twentieth century, college football was a regional pursuit. The ultimate goal for Woody Hayes and Bo Schembechler was to go to the Rose Bowl. Winning it was a secondary pursuit. In twenty seasons at Michigan, Schembechler never captured a national title or completed a perfect season, yet his ability to win or share thirteen Big Ten championships made him an infallible legend. His 5-12 bowl record was ignored.

At Ohio State, Hayes went 2-6 in his final eight bowl appearances and "nobody cared," Helwagen said. "It was, 'My God, the man is a legend.'" In Jim Tressel's first decade coaching Ohio State, he went 9-1 against Michigan, won a share of six consecutive Big Ten championships, and made six straight BCS bowl games. And yet when the Buckeyes lost three of them in a row, "there [was] an undercurrent of disillusion," Helwagen said. "Now they've seen there is something out there, a brighter star to reach for. And when you don't get it, they're upset. They don't understand."

Pre-Internet, the idea of a split national title was frustrating but at least passable. Though the two national opinion polls—the AP and the coaches'—might choose different teams as champions, each school could hold a parade and pretend the other didn't exist. If there was a geographical separation—Miami, Florida, is closer to Bolivia than to the University of Washington, with which it split the 1991 title—fan interaction was minimal.

The Internet has made the world smaller, and no matter how segmented the college football universe, it's ultimately woven like wicker. Everyone has access to everyone else. Used to be that like-minded fans could comfort one another in break rooms at work or dorm lounges after a loss. Rival fans today don't bother waiting until the game is over to commence the trash talk. The ability to heckle takes one click and a few keystrokes.

The Superfans' relentlessness caused a shift in expectations and drove college football's supersizing: bigger coaching salaries, better facilities, and larger conferences, all to help chase the influx of money. Tradition means nothing in the pursuit of money to feed the beast. Coaches have tried to match the intensity, meet the demands of the job, and now only the strongest and most committed survive. The dadgum days of Bobby Bowden, who retired from Florida State in 2009, have given way to a generation of workaholic robo-coaches such as Urban Meyer, who worked himself into the hospital at Florida before stepping down after six seasons at just forty-six years old. Nothing is the same in the post-Internet world, and no one should bother claiming as much.

Except the Cartel tries. Rather than understanding and accommodating the growing ranks of Superfans, they've chosen to paint them as crazies, dismiss them as unimportant, or plain ignore their passion.

Hancock still believes that fans will accept the BCS's failures as an agree-to-disagree fact of life. Instead, he has become the face of the Cartel's misguided social-media campaign, routinely ridiculed by fans for his illogical, aw-shucks radio interviews and the BCS's mind-numbing Twitter posts that don't seem to understand the basic tenets of modern corporate community engagement. As *Advertising Age* lectured the BCS: "If you know your product is universally loathed, Twitter is not the place for you."

The third post of the BCS's first official Twitter feed, @INSIDEtheBCS, cited a quote from Meyer calling the BCS "not perfect, but it has been great for college football." Hancock forgot to point out that when Meyer coached Utah, he told the *New York Times*, "The system is a failure."

Fans raged against the Twitter feed and its equally ridiculous Web companion, PlayoffProblem.com. One Twitter user signed up for an account, typed out a one-line blast—*@INSIDEtheBCS We hate you. Signed, Everyone. Thank you.*—and never posted again. Hundreds of comments trashing the BCS littered its antiplayoff website on which it tried to argue with opponents. About a year after its inception, @INSIDEtheBCS was shuttered for a new account: @everygamecounts. No one ever said the BCS was beyond false advertising.

The social-media failures merely highlight the dawn of a smarter fan. Enough factual information floats around the Web that fans willing to inform themselves can find the proper sources to do so. The backlash signals that more and more are doing so. When a ten-minute radio interview produces countless message board threads, not to mention wall-to-wall calls on talk shows around the country, it's not the sign of a branding snafu. It's a problem that runs to the core of the product.

"The fans are more educated," Burton said. "The more personally you buy in to the game, the more you read, the more you follow it, the deeper you get into something and the more personal involvement you have. Then when the BCS is screwing with your team, it is screwing with you."

The Cartel asks generations of fans obsessed with near-daily advancement in their world to support the ineffective, old way. The Cartel tells consumers who have wrested control that they might as well go along with the current structure because some faceless men sitting in an ivory tower say so. The Cartel wants the people who spend their paychecks and devote their time to be satisfied with an old-fashioned congratulatory slap on the back for the 12-0 regular season that, for whatever reason, just isn't good enough.

And when it realizes none of that works, the Cartel will find itself confronted by a great lesson of the Internet age: The product always bows to the masses, not the other way around.

16 All in a *GameDay*'s Work

If college football is a religion, then its weekly service is a two-hour, nationally televised revival featuring four preachers and a swarming mass of worshippers who hang on every word (when they're not too busy draining a beer from their tailgate).

Each Saturday morning at 10 A.M. ET, outside a frenzied stadium, ESPN's *College GameDay* pregame show reminds college football's flock of all that is sacred and worthwhile about the sport. This is the Superfan's spiritual nourishment, a program that counts millions of viewers nationwide, thousands on-set, and, perhaps, one high above. In 2000, *GameDay* analyst Lee Corso picked Georgia Tech to defeat Virginia Tech at Lane Stadium, the Hokies' home field. Moments later, a lightning bolt singed his rental car. "I don't know what a Hokie is," Corso said, "but God is one of 'em."

Amid the divinity stands a false idol. The Cartel likes to claim the growth of college football over the past decade is directly due to the BCS. God knows, as does any Hokie, Bruin, Aggie, Razorback, Panther, or Badger, that television is as responsible as anything. Whether it's the pageantry of *GameDay* or the expansion of coverage to provide noon-to-night action on Saturday and games almost every day of the week, TV has helped college football evolve into a behemoth—one that outgrew the BCS long ago.

GameDay pushed televised college football coverage beyond the on-field action and took fans on a coast-to-coast carnival ride. It didn't just show games. It showcased the sport: the culture, the tradition, the passion, and the fun—one campus, one mascot head, one debate at a time.

Saturday morning used to be for cartoons. Now, an entire generation has grown up watching *GameDay*, and television's impact on college football's evolution is direct and tangible. A regional pastime morphed into a national frenzy. Recruiting boundaries faded. Respect and recognition no longer tied themselves to history and location. Anger bubbled over a paternalistic championship system in which the Cartel claimed to know what and who is best. The Internet and television grew in tandem, played off each other, and created a groundswell the Cartel can't stop.

"No question it's a different sport," said John Wildhack, ESPN's vice president for programming, who worked on *GameDay* in the early 1990s. "It's far more popular, it's bigger, it's better, and the depth is remarkable, compared to where it was fifteen, twenty years ago. In the mid-1990s, there may have been eight to ten blue-chip programs. Now you can go thirty, thirty-five teams deep."

Which doesn't exactly match up with a system that haphazardly selects two teams and deems them the best. Life would be so much easier for the Cartel had the *GameDay* crew not figured out how to go beyond the highlights and connect with the sport's lifeblood.

Back in 1993, *GameDay* was a quality studio show with great on-set chemistry. Host Chris Fowler served as referee between the strong, educated opinions of a former coach, Corso, and a former player, Craig James. But it didn't channel college football's excitement, because three guys wearing suits in a Connecticut studio never could convey the pre-kickoff energy of Clemson's

Death Valley or the color of the Volunteer Navy on the Tennessee River or the beauty of the Flatirons above Folsom Field in Boulder, Colorado. As anyone who has attended a college game knows, only half the action occurs on the field.

When No. 1 Florida State and No. 2 Notre Dame were on a collision course for a November 1993 showdown, ESPN wondered about dropping *GameDay* down by Touchdown Jesus. The enthusiasm of a South Bend Saturday could seep into the broadcast, transporting new viewers along with it. There were logistical risks, of course. This was live TV. Soon enough, everyone agreed it was worth the gamble, and by 1994, ESPN no longer could confine *GameDay* to a studio.

Seventeen years later, the show is a traveling extravaganza, complete with its own RV, an on-site crew seventy-five strong, screaming minions in every city, and a quartet of hosts who are treated like rock stars: Fowler, Corso, Kirk Herbstreit, and Desmond Howard need a security detail to get to and from the set. Their cell phones blow up with coaches begging them to bring the show to their campus for what's considered a two-hour recruiting infomercial and the ultimate stamp of legitimacy. The show expanded in 2010, adding an hour at 9 A.M. on ESPNU with host Erin Andrews, who tends to ensure crowds will arrive early.

GameDay anchors ESPN's concept of turning each week of the season into episodic TV, an amalgam of action, drama, and suspense. The Superfan gets up in the morning with word on the possible plot developments and can stay until midnight for *College Football Final*, a lively in-studio recap featuring host Rece Davis and analysts Mark May and Lou Holtz. The day turns into an experience, a chance to live vicariously through fans who migrate from a party-filled quad to the *GameDay* set to the stadium and back home to soak in another game or two.

Campuses come alive when *GameDay* arrives. In 1996, Corso

began donning a mascot head to signify his final prediction for the on-site game, and he finds himself the most popular or vilified man in town every week depending on which team he chooses. Superfans wake up at 6 A.M. to stake out a spot so they can cheer or boo Corso's choice of mascot head. With cameras trained on the crowds, signs both colorful and off-color began sprouting up, one-upmanship always encouraged.

It's such an event that fans of teams not even playing in that day's game show up. In 2003, a Washington State alum named Tom Pounds drove eight hundred miles from his home in Albuquerque, New Mexico, to fly a dark red Cougars flag among the crowd in Austin, Texas. Two weeks later, he shipped "Ol' Crimson" to another Wazzu alum who drove to a *GameDay* broadcast in Madison, Wisconsin. It got forwarded to Ohio, then Oklahoma, and on and on. There hasn't been a *GameDay* since without either Ol' Crimson or its companion, Ol' White— and sometimes both—flying in the background, a streak that reached 104 games in 2010.

"If we were doing this for the NBA or the NFL or even college basketball, it wouldn't have the same feel," said Herbstreit, the former Ohio State quarterback who replaced James in 1996 just as the show began heading out weekly. "In college football, the fan bases are so passionate and authentic. That's the difference. We don't tell them, 'OK, now you cheer.' There is no applause sign. We're in the middle of a tailgate on these college campuses, and we just have to turn the camera on amidst all these [meat] smokers and tailgates and people. It's like, 'OK, let's set up there.' And it's all around us."

So whether it's windy, rainy, snowy, freezing, scorching, or humid, *GameDay* shows up. It doesn't discriminate where, either. The crew has traveled to an Ivy League game; another between historically black colleges, the Division III Amherst-

Williams rivalry; and all three service academies. With *Game-Day* familiarizing places big and small, nowhere is too far away, no coach too obscure, no campus town anonymous. The college football world shrinks by the year.

When it first formed the BCS, the Cartel could get away with telling the fans which teams were and weren't worthy of championship consideration. There were often fewer than ten games on TV a week, forcing fans to trust panels of sportswriters or coaches or computers. Now the games are wall-to-wall, two to three dozen a week on ESPN's various platforms alone. Then there's CBS, NBC, Versus, and Fox Sports regional outlets. The Big Ten created its own television network, in part to assure its lesser teams airtime. The Pac-12 and some Big 12 schools plan to do the same. In 2011, the University of Texas, in conjunction with ESPN, created its own Longhorn Network, which has caught the attention of other major schools, such as Oklahoma, and will likely be duplicated.

"There's a vacuum right now for programming," Texas AD DeLoss Dodds said. "There's not enough programming and a lot of companies out there that want programming."

In the 1990s, fans in the Midwest might tune in to the Rose Bowl to see what kind of team USC had. Now they've watched eight or nine Trojans games live. Anyone can scout a smaller-conference school and believe in its ability or dismiss its credentials. The opinion is self-generated and unfiltered, a direct descendant of *GameDay*'s democratic view.

Of course, despite how big *GameDay* and the Internet have made college football, the TV ratings for some of the biggest postseason games remain mediocre, a direct indictment of the one-off nature of the bowl system and the inability of the BCS to deliver the compelling matchups it idly promises. Aside from the title game and the Rose Bowl, which benefits from a 5 P.M.

ET time slot on New Year's Day, bowl games rarely are broadcast ratings hits.

The ratings for each game dipped in 2011, when ESPN televised them instead of broadcast networks. The 2011 Rose Bowl had an 11.3 rating, with the Sugar (8.2), Orange Bowl (6.7), and Fiesta (6.2) following.

In 2011, the NFL playoffs set record after record. All four wild-card games beat the BCS title broadcast. Their average (18.1 to 15.3) was 18.3 percent higher. In the divisional round, the ratings leapt into the 20s, with the New York Jets–New England Patriots game posting a 26.2. The conference championship round spiked into the 30s. The Super Bowl drew a 51.1 rating, good for 111 million viewers, the most in American television history. It's not just the NFL's popularity. Playoffs, with their eminently more important games, come with the requisite intrigue to draw diehards and casual fans alike.

The month-or-so layoff between the end of the regular season and the BCS bowls slays any momentum from conference championship games, and the one-and-done structure of the BCS prevents an exciting game from carrying over. The last Orange Bowl played to an audience no doubt enthralled by the play of Stanford quarterback Andrew Luck. Rather than tune in the following week and see more, Luck converts would have to wait nine months. "With a playoff you have week-to-week, [so] the hype is huge," Dodds said. "You don't have that in the bowl system. You play and everyone goes home." In the NCAA basketball tournament, obscure players, such as Davidson's Stephen Curry in 2008, can become overnight stars and singular reasons to watch.

The event can take on a life of its own. In 2010, low-profile Butler, a small private school from Indianapolis, reached the men's national title game against Duke. Rather than hurt the ratings, the game produced the most viewers since 1997, according to CBS. The audience was up 31 percent over the 2009 title game between name opponents North Carolina and Michigan State. That's the power of a dream-big, lose-and-go-home tournament.

Considering the endless press releases touting television ratings "success," the Cartel's standards are low. It wasn't just BCS games that lagged in the ratings. ESPN's non-BCS bowls were down 9 percent in 2010, according to Nielsen. Though no American sport matches the NFL in terms of fan interest, college football lags proportionally further behind pro football than college basketball does behind the NBA. Today's college football ratings are Lilliputian next to those potentially drawn by playoff match-ups culminating in a true national championship game.

A playoff, current and former television executives said, would be an enormous success because it is an interconnected series of events that plays so well to mega-corporations versed in promotion across different mediums. Football, even more than basketball, is perfectly built to capture the fair-weather audience. The week off between games allows for back stories to be told, predictions to be made, and casual fans to catch up on what they missed.

"The snowball momentum of a playoff would build to a crescendo of interest that's never been seen in college football," said Ben Goss, an associate professor of sports marketing at Missouri State. "The ratings would follow."

Estimated one current sports television executive: "The semi-finals would do what the current title game does, high teens. The championship game, at that point, is a big-time television event, mid-20s at least."

ESPN has done its part to grow not just ratings but the entire sport, something of limited interest to the BCS. Taking *GameDay* on the road is an expensive production, and ESPN executives admit they could turn a greater profit by returning the show to the studio, even if the ratings dipped. But they know better than to risk ruining a franchise by chasing a few dollars.

College football is too important to the network. For years, the SEC had near-exclusive rights to ESPN's Saturday prime-time slot, a crown jewel of promotion. There was perhaps no better way to sell Southern football than in packed stadiums under the lights on national TV. When ESPN expanded its Saturday night offerings to showcase non-SEC games on ABC and ESPN2, Mike Slive, the SEC commissioner, was furious. He called ESPN's home base in Bristol, Connecticut and, as he put it, began "ranting and raving."

"[It] appeared to me to be intuitively a competitive situation and not necessarily good for us," Slive said. "And they said to me, 'Your ratings will go up.' And I said, 'No way.'"

ESPN was right. By counterprogramming college football with even more college football, everyone's ratings went up, even the conference that used to have a monopoly on the time slot.

"We did a lot of research," said Wildhack, the ESPN executive. "The average fan watches forty minutes of a three-hour game. So the diehard fan is watching all three hours of their team, but there are a lot of people that are surfing in and out of games. So if we can navigate that audience by updating what's happening in other games, we can move them between our networks. Giving them as much choice as possible, there seems to be an insatiable appetite for college football in this country."

And no conference better illustrates that than the SEC, which has maximized the power of television. Over the last twenty years, the conference has left behind its local roots and expanded like a big-box franchise. Everyone knows the SEC, and it's hard not to appreciate a conference that has won five straight national championships. CBS and ESPN paid a combine $3 billion to televise SEC games for fifteen years.

In 2009, CBS's national broadcast of the SEC game of the week actually drew larger audiences than ABC's regional broadcasts of other conferences, which showed local teams in their home markets. The SEC was beating other leagues in their own backyards. It is almost NFL Lite—its coaches and players outsize personalities, its controversies full of staying power and resonance. You didn't need to live in the South to have an opinion about Tim Tebow, who was the story of the 2010 NFL Draft even as he went to Denver with the 25th overall pick. A year later, the combination of Cam Newton's on-field prowess and off-field soap opera dominated the season's storyline. The allegations of a pay-for-play scheme didn't prevent the Auburn quarterback from winning the Heisman Trophy and a national championship.

"We have become a national brand," Slive said.

The expansion of television coverage—and the information delivered by *GameDay* and ESPN's other shows—has likewise changed the recruiting game. Top players consider schools beyond the brand-name programs because they can see the offense and defense and get a sense of the crowd and hear the fight song from thousands of miles away. No longer do players resist attending a school two time zones from their homes. And the talent has leveled out accordingly.

"It's no longer a regional sport," Herbstreit said. "It's become a national deal where everyone is dialed in. You have to be dialed in to every game. Because of that I think the popularity is greater than it ever has been."

Herbstreit owns a front-row seat to the hysteria, and he need only turn around and see the zoo behind him. *GameDay*'s ratings are bigger, its crowds bolder. Week after week, the show connects a nation of fans to the pulse of college football. More hype. More parity. More anticipation.

College football is a made-for-TV mega-power, and ESPN

understands it's the perfect conduit through which the sport can proselytize to the masses. The BCS doesn't. The current system captures none of the emotion, the hope, the possibility, the atmosphere. It's not an event. It's not something that excites people. It's a cold, calculating, governing bureaucracy—the tax man of sports.

It's black and white in a pastime whose growth is perhaps best personified by a bright primary color in the unlikeliest of places.

17 Blue Turf vs. Blue Blood

Gene Bleymaier was thirty-two when divine inspiration struck, quite literally, out of the blue. Because he had already been the athletic director at Boise State University for four years, he didn't flinch at walking into the school president's office with his biggest, boldest, craziest idea yet, perfect for the upstart program he was building in Idaho's capital.

Blue turf.

It was a forward-thinking, big-dreaming concept that symbolizes one of the BCS's problems: the rise of the nobody. When the Cartel designed the BCS in the mid-1990s, such small-conference programs as Boise State, TCU, Utah, Houston, and Fresno State might as well have not existed. The Cartel built the BCS to strengthen college football's longtime power structure. It deemed members of the six major conferences legitimate and everyone else not. Even among those conferences, there was a clear delineation between the elite and unworthy. The premise was born of the Cartel's never-ending paternalism: It knows who plays real football and who doesn't, and any team that succeeds outside the power structure deserves a nice little pinch on its cute cheek.

And then along came Boise State.

It started with Bleymaier's crazy idea, one not even he could possibly have seen as the harbinger of an anonymous, out-of-the-way program crashing two Fiesta Bowls and winning both. The school's modest Bronco Stadium playing surface was green back then, just like everyone else's. That was the problem, Bleymaier figured. If you've got a I-AA football program, in Idaho no less, with aspirations of grandeur, you can't afford to be just like everyone else. If you wait around for the rest of the country to notice you, it won't.

Bleymaier thought he had a sleeping giant in Boise. The school was growing fast. Two decades earlier, it had been a junior college. The city was Idaho's largest—beautiful and surprisingly cosmopolitan—and the metropolitan population of a quarter million would more than double over the next twenty years. This wasn't some tiny, cornfield-surrounded college town. Locals were desperate for a sports program to support. There were Fortune 500 companies to tap.

He just needed a hook, something to make people locally, regionally, and nationally not only notice Boise State but remember it. The green turf was old, so Bleymaier found a company that would install the new carpet for $750,000, regardless of color.

"The idea came to me that there is no reason why the field is green," Bleymaier said. "We're not fooling anyone. They know it's not grass. So why should it be green? Why not make it our school colors? When you go to Lincoln, Nebraska, everything is red but the field. When you go to Knoxville, Tennessee, everything is orange but the field. So we said, 'Hey, come to Boise and you'll see blue.'"

Boise State president John Keiser was convinced, except for one hitch: He worried that the blue turf would be an aesthetic disaster. While the company could do blue, it had never deviated from green. It couldn't even offer a picture of what the field might look like. Bleymaier improvised, turning the tint on his old TV toward blue and creating a reasonable facsimile.

Boise State took the plunge in 1986, and the turf was a hit. Fans loved it. Players, too. The program moved to Division I-A in 1996, its Smurf Turf already a cult legend. Travelers along I-84 often stopped to take pictures of the turf around which apocryphal stories blossomed. One said before the lines and logos were painted on the field, birds and ducks mistook the turf for a pond, which they dive-bombed to their ultimate demise. Bleymaier, ever the promoter, always understanding the value of publicity—even in the form of crazy lore that might retroactively offend PETA—keeps the legend alive with his hemming and hawing.

"I can neither confirm nor deny that report," he said, laughing.

Faraway television executives were intrigued by the gimmick and soon found that when they threw the blue turf on television, remote controls stopped mid-click. Maybe it was out of curiosity, but fans stayed and watched.

Soon it wasn't just the field that made them dizzy. Boise State went for it on fourth and long, saw two-point conversions as an opportunity, and regularly spread the field with five wide receivers. In the late 1990s, few took Boise State seriously, but damn if they weren't fun to watch. People did, and the high ratings meant more TV games. The Broncos played on weeknights, late nights—basically anytime ESPN asked, figuring a scheduling inconvenience here and there would pay dividends in recruiting.

"People who were progressive thinkers saw the advantage of weeknight games," said John Wildhack, ESPN's vice president of programming. "We've got a philosophy at ESPN: Any team can play their way on. Boise hasn't only played their way on, they've stayed on."

In 2009, the Broncos played eight times in nationally televised games, making them one of the most visible teams in the country. They also won more games in the 2000s than any other team—with five undefeated regular seasons—captured seven Western Athletic Conference championships, and, over that span, posted a 55-1 conference record.

The program's moment of glory came in the 2007 Fiesta Bowl, when ultra-underdog Boise State beat storied Oklahoma on a series of late-game trick plays called by never-rattled coach Chris Petersen. The final score came on a daring two-point conversion in overtime courtesy of a Statue of Liberty play to running back Ian Johnson.

Minutes later, with Fox's Chris Myers calling the play-by-play, Johnson proposed to his cheerleader girlfriend, Chrissy Popadics, on national television. She said yes.

You couldn't make this stuff up.

The game is considered one of the most famous and exciting in college football history, and it quickly became a recurring nightmare for the Cartel. Boise State had the nation buzzing. The Broncos were 13-0, the only undefeated team in America. Football fans pined to see what else Petersen kept in his book of magic tricks. The rest of the country wanted to know more about Johnson and his cheerleader fiancée. *Good Morning America*, *Entertainment Tonight*, and *People* magazine called. Hollywood agents wanted to pitch the couple on TV shows and movie scripts. Almost everybody agreed: These giant killers deserved another game. And of course they didn't get one.

Americans are trained to watch sports through the prism of a playoff. Win and keep playing. When George Mason, a commuter school in suburban Washington, D.C., upset powerhouse Michigan State in the opening round of the 2006 NCAA men's basketball tournament, it didn't congratulate itself and call it a season. Everyone got to watch as the Patriots took on mighty North Carolina two nights later. They won again. Two games later, they beat Connecticut to advance to the Final Four. By then, George Mason was the nation's darling, only to be supplanted four years later by Butler and its back-to-back championship game appearances.

It took the same amount of time for Boise State to follow up its Fiesta Bowl triumph with something of equal import. The milestone win over Oklahoma so shifted the paradigm of college football that when the Broncos returned to the Fiesta Bowl in 2010, fans were irate. Rather than face TCU, the Mountain West's undefeated entry, Boise State wanted to overwhelm another big-conference opponent. The game was dubbed the "Separate but Equal Bowl" by *Sports Illustrated*'s Andy Staples. Rep. Jim Matheson (D-Utah) went one step further: "The Kids' Table Bowl."

Boise State had gone from not being good enough for a BCS game to a BCS game not being good enough for Boise State. Blue turf was turning blue blood.

For the Cartel, Boise's success wasn't something to celebrate. The BCS's exclusionary practices work only if it can convince the public that teams from non–big six conferences are so weak and lowly that their gaudy, unbeaten records are specters. The Cartel's best way to suppress demand for fair bowl access or a full-on playoff is through a campaign of disrespect, a case that thins by the day.

"They really do look down on Hawaii or Utah," a current television executive said. "They don't want to be on the same field as them. In the same vicinity."

The Cartel wants fans to believe that any non–big six conference team that happens to achieve a modicum of success is simply a shooting star that ought be ignored. It prefers the one-year glory of the Ball State Cardinals, a long-suffering program that streaked to a 12-0 regular-season record in 2008, threatened to sneak into the BCS, and reverted the next year with seven consecutive losses to open the season. Ball State was a nice story and no real threat on the national stage. Such flukes happen.

The Boise States of the world are different. They keep building and getting better. They hit the milepost of any major athletic program in 2011: The NCAA cited them for lack of institutional control, including secondary violations in football, which led to Bleymaier's dismissal. Later in the year, they would leave behind the WAC for the more competitive Mountain West. It's no different than Utah, the original BCS buster in 2005. It went 12-0 that year and beat Big East champion Pittsburgh in the Fiesta Bowl behind coach Urban Meyer. When Meyer left for Florida, everyone figured the Utes would go away. The school hired another dynamic coach, Kyle Whittingham, who just four seasons later had put together an even better Utah team that went 13-0 in 2008 and beat Alabama 31–17 in the Sugar Bowl, part of its current nine-game bowl winning streak. In the ultimate sign of respect, the Utes will join the renamed Pac-12 in 2011, the outcast bullying its way into the in crowd.

Meanwhile, Brigham Young, a storied program with a national title and a Heisman Trophy winner, hired Bronco Mendenhall and saw its program return to prominence. The Cougars followed Notre Dame's lead following the 2010 season and left the Mountain West to become a national independent. Down at Texas Christian, coach Gary Patterson began fully mining the talent-rich Metroplex region and churned out 10-win season after 10-win season. As a kid in rural Kansas, Patterson worked endless hours leveling farmland for the family business. As a coach, he built, proving the Horned Frogs were more than just LaDainian Tomlinson.

In 2008, TCU produced more NFL Draft selections than any other program in the state of Texas—more than Texas, Texas

Tech, or Texas A&M. Not that it mattered to Patterson, who returned such tremendous talent that TCU finished the 2009 regular season 12-0 and made its first BCS bowl. A year later it went 13-0, won the Rose Bowl, and had five players drafted, compared to the Longhorns' four and one apiece from the Red Raiders and Aggies. Immediately following the regular season, TCU began a $105 million reconstruction project that the school said would turn Amon G. Carter Stadium into "the Camden Yards of college football." In 2012, the Horned Frogs will join the Big East, no longer some upstart.

Big-time programs no longer need to ride the coattails of their own history. The schools have poured money into facilities. They've upped recruiting budgets and marketing. They've kept improving. Meyer, even after getting to Florida, said a school such as Utah has far more built-in advantages, including quality of city, than some BCS-level universities in smaller states or tiny towns.

"When we're able to get kids to visit, we have a very high success rate to get kids to commit," Whittingham said. "That's the key for us. Get recognized, get exposure, and get kids willing to come and take a look. We can recruit speed and athleticism here."

Utah's 13-0 season in 2008 was powered by skill-position players who came from California or Texas. All were African Americans starring at the flagship university in a state that's nearly 93 percent white. That's college football today.

If Boise State relied on Idaho talent alone, it never would have left I-AA. In 2009, players hailed from all over the West, including thirty-five from California. The Broncos' best cornerback, NFL first-round pick Kyle Wilson, was from Piscataway, New Jersey. Like Whittingham, Petersen believes if he can get a kid to visit Boise, he can get him to commit. And the Broncos' near-decade-long dominance—they've managed the third-most

BCS bowl appearances among West Coast teams despite their conference affiliation—reinforces that a talent diaspora indeed exists.

The explosion in media coverage means that recruits in California, Florida, and Texas no longer tolerate waiting for playing time behind established upperclassmen at brand-name schools. Not only does ESPN beam in games from all over the country, but the Internet provides extensive national media coverage and the ability for players to easily research and follow distant teams. They don't need to take an unofficial visit with Dad to see a school's weight room. There's a video tour on its website.

On YouTube, kids market themselves with highlight videos they hope pique the interest of a coach who otherwise may not have scouted them. One more click takes a player to Facebook, MySpace, Twitter, and any number of social-networking sites that allow young prospects to keep in touch. In the 1990s, top high school players may have attended a local summer camp where they would befriend other stars from the area and, quite often, plot their college choices together. Now, with regional talent camps run by Rivals.com, Reebok, and others, a quarterback from Orlando is friends with a lineman from Minnesota, and they text each other about playing together in Virginia.

"When I was in high school, I lived in the [southwestern] part of Ohio," said ESPN's Kirk Herbstreit, a highly recruited quarterback from suburban Dayton in 1988 who chose Ohio State. "You barely knew anything about the northeast part of the state. . . . No school is far away anymore."

Consider the state of Oregon, a mostly rural place with fewer than 4 million residents. It's best known for producing long-distance runners, not football players. Nike, the state's ubiquitous company, was created when the founders, including Phil Knight, made running shoe soles in waffle irons. They didn't know anything about football.

Historically, Oregon and Oregon State have been nonfactors in the Pac-10 title chase. Without a strong local talent base, they could never compete with USC, UCLA, or Washington. For years, college recruiting was a numbers game. Now they do it the way Boise has, getting what they can from their home area and recruiting relentlessly in other ZIP codes. Oregon and Oregon State took the ethos of the Internet and modern-day TV—boundaries no longer exist—and applied it to their recruiting efforts. The uniform—different from week to week, custom designed by Nike, and special to the Ducks—may say Oregon, but the roster says something else. The schools draw out-of-state athletes with superior facilities, coaches, support, and way of life. There's a reason USC has lost a game to a team from the state of Oregon for the last six years.

At the end of the 2009 season, Oregon and Oregon State played their annual Civil War game, this time for the Pac-10 title. Oregon won thanks to huge performances from running backs LaMichael James (hometown: Texarkana, Texas) and LeGarrette Blount (Perry, Florida), quarterback Jeremiah Masoli (Daly City, California), and wide receiver Jeff Maehl (Paradise, California). That was enough to offset the brilliant play of Oregon State running back Jacquizz Rodgers (Richmond, Texas), quarterback Sean Canfield (Carlsbad, California), and linebacker Keaton Kristick (Fountain Hills, Arizona).

"That's how it's changed," Herbstreit said. "Two running backs from Texas, in a high-profile game, between two teams in Oregon that fringe fans would say, 'Who, what?' The fans don't know who the coaches are. The high school players, however, now know everything about these schools."

In Oregon's 2011 BCS title game appearance, not a single Duck who gained a yard on offense, intercepted a pass, or returned a punt or kick hailed from the state.

No matter how hard it tries, the Cartel no longer can brush

off programs from the fringes of the power conferences or the top of the non–big six leagues. "Some teams just slip by with votes," said former Georgia wide receiver A. J. Green. "I think those teams like TCU deserve to play for the national championship, even if their conference isn't as strong."

The fans have seen too many teams the Cartel claims are unworthy prove otherwise. Only the BCS still lives in its 1990s cocoon, where it discounts a team based on conference affiliation and home-state population or location. Everyone else knows better. They know the level of play in college football, with burgeoning dynasties at Boise State and Oregon and TCU, is better than it used to be.

It's as clear as the blue turf.

18 The Civil War

The Cartel absorbs attacks on a daily basis from, among others, fans, radio hosts, newspaper columnists, congressmen, and coaches. Out of the public view, it must fend off another threat, one far more acute and capable of breaking up the whole racket: itself.

Don't let its outward solidarity fool you. The BCS today is Hatfield vs. Hatfield, a system in a constant state of civil war, assaulted from within by feuding factions from conferences whose motivations dovetail less and less, according to a number of sources familiar with the strife. The BCS exists because the men in power didn't want to lose their conferences' stranglehold on money and influence, and as the landscape of college football shifts, so do their motivations.

Conferences are built to compete against each other, not cooperate and sing "Kumbaya." There are egos, rivalries, and backstabbing. Commissioners have no misgivings about playing wild-game hunter and poaching schools from other conferences. They squeeze every dollar, even if it endangers their so-called partners. Their opposition to changing the BCS is as much a product of self-serving inaction as anything. Truth is, while the Cartel defends the BCS, almost no one is satisfied with its current incarnation.

Mike Slive, the commissioner of the SEC, is among the

brightest and most well-regarded athletic administrators in the country. A onetime district court judge in New Hampshire, Slive was stung by the 2004 season when the BCS left his conference's unbeaten champion, Auburn, out of the title game. He decided to advocate a fairer plan for college football. "If you love the game, the goal is to help the game, not hurt the game," he said.

He and his staff spent two years crafting a comprehensive plan for a plus-one, the modest four-team playoff. Rather than endorsing a complete overhaul, he suggested a tweak that would leave the bowl system intact and generate another boatload of money for college football.

This was no big-dreaming fan with a wild plan. This was no Conference USA president claiming his team deserved a shot. This was the man in the middle of the Cartel, the head of the supercharged SEC. He certainly couldn't be accused of self-interest. At the time, SEC teams were 4-0 in BCS title games and had won consecutive championships. Despite the Auburn disaster, if anyone was benefiting from the system, it was Mike Slive.

He came with the support of a number of his own university presidents, including Bernie Machen of the University of Florida and Michael Adams of the University of Georgia. ACC commissioner John Swofford and a number of that league's presidents, including Florida State's T. K. Wetherell, were also on board.

In the spring of 2008, Slive took his idea to the annual BCS meetings in Florida and laid it out to the other ten conference commissioners and the athletic director of Notre Dame.

Within a matter of hours, his proposal was dead. Slive's supposed Cartel allies—commissioners from the Big East, Big Ten, Big 12, and Pac-10—blocked its path. It didn't come up for a vote, in part because "we never vote," as one commissioner said. Five people in the room willing to make an estimate say it would have passed 8-4. The four big conferences that opposed the plan refused to even take it back to their respective presidents for discussion. Their stated fear: The plus-one might prove too popular and profitable and ultimately expand into an eight- or sixteen-team playoff.

"We felt like there could be . . . more pressure to add more teams with an ability to get to the national championship game," Big 12 commissioner Dan Beebe said.

Perhaps this was comeuppance for fourteen years earlier, when Vince Dooley, the former Georgia football coach and AD, walked into the SEC meetings hoping to affect change and the conference brass put up an obstructionist barricade. With Slive, the Cartel hadn't merely snuffed out one of its own. It rebuked him in public for daring to step out of line. The ruling majority deemed something on which Slive had worked for two years unworthy of even a debate. When the SEC went on to win BCS championship games in 2009, '10, and '11 and ran its streak to five straight, conference staffers enjoyed a chuckle.

"This is a marathon and not a sprint," Slive said. There would be more fights to come, more dissatisfaction seeding itself throughout the system. The Cartel loves a good brawl. Unlike so many other fights it wages, this one didn't cost a penny.

The BCS hired two men in 2009 to shield itself from the grenades lobbed its way daily. Executive director Bill Hancock takes the public floggings and Ari Fleischer works behind the scenes. To buttress their work, the BCS surreptitiously aims to stave off congressional intervention and keep its stranglehold alive with an old quarterback who tries to navigate Washington, D.C., as well as he did the wishbone offense.

When J. C. Watts joined the BCS's payroll in 2003, he brought gravitas to the political and college football worlds. After four consecutive terms as the U.S. Representative from

Oklahoma's 4th District, Watts left the House to start a lobbying firm. His success running the University of Oklahoma's offense from 1979 to 1981 gave him credibility to a group that needed a Washington rainmaker.

Watts was known for his tough, fearless, trailblazing ways. He grew up impoverished in rural Oklahoma and was one of the first black students to integrate his elementary school. Originally the Sooners' seventh-string quarterback, Watts soon ascended to the top of the depth chart and led Barry Switzer's offense with panache. In 1994, running as a Republican, Watts won a seat in the House. He voted to impeach Bill Clinton, refused to join the Congressional Black Caucus, and responded to catcalls of "Uncle Tom" by labeling his critics "race-hustling poverty pimps." Watts never felt a need to apologize for what he believed.

Then the Cartel hired him. Between 2003 and 2010, the BCS paid $740,000 to Watts's lobbying firm, J. C. Watts Companies, according to the Center for Responsive Politics. It bought some political pull, if not Watts' public approval.

"I don't advise the BCS on whether they should or shouldn't have a playoff," he told *USA Today* in 2009, declining to take a stance on the issue. "I just kind of help them navigate getting through the hearings and what to expect and how to prepare themselves."

Expensive tour guides are a Washington staple, and it was inevitable that college football would enter the netherworld of profiteers who subsist off confusion, conflict, and coarse debate. Political involvement draws lobbyists, and with billions of dollars in public money at stake—not to mention an easy way to gain the votes of impassioned fans—the politicians can't resist.

It isn't easy to shoo Congress away when the athletic departments of the ninety-nine public schools in Division I-A needed a combined $826 million in subsidies just to balance their books in 2008, according to *USA Today*. The number rose 20 percent the last three years, and it's not going to stop. If the system wants to waste taxpayer money, it can't easily complain when politicians start asking where it goes. Good idea or not, Washington is now forever involved.

The political movement began in 2003 when Tulane president Scott Cowen, eyeing an annual $7 million budget shortfall in his athletic department, announced he would consider dropping his school's football team to Division III. Tulane fans decried the idea, and some called for Cowen's ouster. Wisely, he retreated and instead found a common enemy.

Tulane had gone undefeated in 1998, and as a member of Conference USA, it had no access to the BCS bowls, even with an 11-0 record. Tulane settled for a Liberty Bowl appearance, and five years later, Cowen drew on the lingering resentment.

He organized forty-four of the fifty-two other non-BCS schools and set out on a media blitz to destroy the BCS. In an op-ed piece published by the *New York Times*, Cowen called on school presidents "to actively challenge the NCAA, the BCS, and the current system of intercollegiate athletics in this country." The non-BCS schools threatened legal action, arguing the postseason system violated antitrust laws. They persuaded influential congressmen to hold hearings on the matter.

Myles Brand, the late president of the NCAA, sprang to mediate the issue. He was adamant that colleges needed to resolve their matters without interference from "external parties." He helped forge a new deal in which the six BCS conferences shared some revenue with the smaller conferences and created a road map for access to BCS bowls and even the title game. The politicians were held at bay.

The Cartel kept its tentacles in Washington anyway. Hogan

Lovells, a D.C.-based law firm that specializes in lobbying, joined the BCS payroll in 2003. "Throughout the world," the company's website reads, "government investigators are stepping up anti-trust enforcement." Where Watts could not reach, Hogan Lovells would. In 2010, the BCS paid $220,000 in lobbying fees to Hogan Lovells, the most it has spent in the nine years the Center for Responsive Politics has tracked its outlay in Washington.

The BCS isn't the only one playing at politics. The same year that the BCS retained Hogan Lovells, the non-BCS schools hired Edelman, a well-known public-relations firm, to polish their message of injustice. Individual schools did their part, too. Purdue and the University of Michigan spent more than $900,000 in lobbying fees, according to federal filings, and one of their objectives was to advocate for the BCS. The ACC and NCAA combined to spend another $370,000 on lobbyists who pressed the issue.

And although Brand's compromise involved increased access, it wasn't enough for the Mountain West. In 2009, it broke ranks and spent $250,000 to hire its own law firm, Arent Fox, which argued that the BCS violates antitrust laws because "competitors cannot, by acting together and with the primary distributors in a market, impose market restraints that guarantee that regardless of the quality of their products, they will receive the vast majority of market revenues and market access. Yet that is exactly what has occurred here under the BCS." One person who agreed was Mark Shurtleff, the three-term Republican attorney general of Utah, who said in the spring of 2011 that he planned to file an antitrust suit against the BCS. Shurtleff urged other state attorney generals to join the case. While opinions were split on whether such a suit will ultimately be successful, some experts suggested it could cost the BCS up to $5 million to defend against while opening itself—and potentially its long-closed books—to the discovery and deposition stages of the case. If nothing else, a state-funded antitrust case would serve as an additional headache.

Leading up to the Department of Justice's letter to the NCAA in 2011 and Shurtleff's threat, the anti-BCS crowd found its greatest ally in an independent group that used the bowls' non-profit status against them. Playoff PAC, a federal political action committee designed to undermine the BCS, became a go-to voice whenever politicians engaged in BCS saber rattling. Created by six football fans in their twenties and thirties—including Matthew Sanderson, a former campaign finance counsel to Sen. John McCain's presidential campaign—Playoff PAC is a part-time endeavor of bipartisan unity, both politically and in the organizers' fandom.

"We have two University of Utah fans, one BYU fan, one University of Texas fan, and one USC fan," Sanderson said. "I don't know who [the sixth member] is a fan of. I think he's just against the BCS on principle. Our organization was created to ratchet up policy and public pressure to change college football."

Playoff PAC has proven the Cartel's worst nightmare. Sanderson's group is relentless: a small, motivated group of highly intelligent, connected lawyers and Washington insiders that works on a shoestring budget courtesy of modest contributions. The BCS has tried to dismiss them repeatedly, yet over and over they've produced press releases and IRS complaints concerning questionable lobbying, exorbitant expenditures, excessive CEO pay, and other embarrassing details. The group's work on the Fiesta Bowl, at first dubbed "old news" by the bowl game, was, along with the relentless reporting of the *Arizona Republic*, the touchstone for ferreting out corruption within the system. Playoff PAC's work runs throughout the Fiesta Bowl's internal report. When the group suggests that similar issues dog other bowl games, only the most naïve ignore them. Sanderson, for one, promises to continue digging.

The fight in Washington is on, evermore money spent on a quandary with a workable resolution. Of course, that needs to start in the back rooms occupied by the Cartel figures who guide college football's future. Right now, the power brokers are too busy gerrymandering their prospects to even know where they'll take it.

For years, the Mountain West and Western Athletic conferences were the two leagues that seemingly would work best together in fighting the BCS. But even they had different approaches to solving the problem. While the WAC wanted to work within the system, the Mountain West not only refused to sign a pending BCS television deal with ESPN/ABC, but it hired Arent Fox, and commissioner Craig Thompson publicly opposed the system in appearances on Capitol Hill. It was a bold act of revolution. The MWC/WAC disagreement mattered little by the end of 2010, when the Mountain West had poached Boise State, Fresno State, Nevada, and Hawaii in hopes of securing an automatic BCS bid.

The other smaller conferences, meanwhile, sat idly and cashed checks from the BCS, content that the system hasn't entirely turned off its spigot. Each of the big six conferences received at least $21.2 million from the 2010–11 BCS pool. The Mountain West, with one team in a BCS game like the Big 12, ACC, and Big East, cashed in just $12.75 million. The WAC earned $4.05 million. The conferences without a team in a BCS game took their payouts—$3.34 million for Conference USA, $2.64 million for the MAC, and $1.94 million for the Sun Belt—and spent another year fantasizing about a playoff and the millions it could guarantee.

The payoffs, particularly to the smallest conferences, amount to figurative hush money—or at least they were supposed to, until Thompson aired his grievances and took public a sliver of the infighting that plagues the BCS.

"I was very disturbed [that] any of our conferences that are part of the BCS [came] out after we negotiated with television and then [proposed] drastic changes to the system," Big 12 commissioner Dan Beebe told the *Dallas Morning News*. "The Mountain West acts like we're holding a gun to their head."

In the wake of all the consternation, tension has increased at the BCS meetings. Factions draw lines and use their political heft to intimidate. "I was out of the room a lot as they discussed me," Thompson said. "I spent more time in the hallway, like a sixth grader."

He wouldn't apologize. He can't. The major conferences received nearly $10 million more than his conference from the BCS despite the same number of teams. And unlike the Big East, at least the Mountain West's entrant, TCU, won its game. One of the Mountain West's attorneys, Alan Fishel, released a chart that showed teams from the Mountain West and WAC bought more tickets and produced higher television ratings for their BCS bowl appearances than teams from the ACC or Big East, yet they received half the revenue. Hancock likes to claim the BCS is primarily about getting the No. 1 and No. 2 teams to meet in bowl game. It's clearly more than that. The inequity forces the Mountain West to do what it can to change the system, Thompson said, while "if you're one of the six automatic qualifying conferences, you don't."

Unless you're Mike Slive. Or John Swofford. Or, really, anyone. Thompson is wrong: Every member of the Cartel will try to change the system if it behooves his conference. The disparate interests and lack of any true leadership—via a college football–wide commissioner who looks out for its well-being—leads to inaction that serves nobody but bowl executives, ADs, and coaches who figured out how to profit off the confusion. The conference commissioners just stand around and argue while the game suffers. No amount of facts seems to get everyone on the same page when it's easier to repeat the empty rhetoric and watch someone else take college football's lunch money.

"Logic doesn't matter," said Texas athletic director DeLoss Dodds, one of the most powerful men in college athletics and a playoff advocate for decades. "We built a system and keep feeding a system that doesn't work.

"We're our own worst enemy."

19 Implicit Trust, Explicit Motivations

Pac-10 commissioner Larry Scott was circling the South Plains in a Raytheon Hawker 800 twin-engine jet like a buzzard about to pick apart what was expected to be the carcass of the Big 12 conference. Colorado already had seceded to the Pac-10. Nebraska had left for the Big Ten. Few thought the league would last another forty-eight hours. It was June 13, 2010, a Sunday, and Scott was puddle jumping from city to city, offering personal invitations to Texas, Texas Tech, Oklahoma, Oklahoma State, and Texas A&M to join a new mega-power: the Pac-16. It would be the first superconference, one that would stretch some 2,500 miles and link cultures as different as the dueling pronunciations and definitions of *rodeo*: Out west, it's a swanky street with an accent. Down south, it's a sport with a twang.

When Tom Hansen retired as commissioner of the Pac-10 in 2009, the league replaced him with Scott, a college sports outsider who previously ran the Women's Tennis Association. He surveyed his new property, wondered how a conference that owned almost the entire West Coast lagged so far behind in revenue, and set out to fix it. Within months, the league's presidents empowered Scott to build a superconference—a profound assault on Hansen's archaic vision of college athletics.

Scott immediately targeted Texas, one of the most storied programs in the country, a revenue behemoth, and, most important, an entrée into an unbeatable market. With the Longhorns in the south and USC out west anchoring a Pac-16 television network, the conference would reap money from the country's two most populous states and a projected 30 million-plus total households. Among the Cartel's heavy hitters, Scott looked like the ultimate leviathan: Within a year of taking over the Pac-10, he was puppeteer for the future of college football.

It took a consortium to cut his strings. As the Pac-10 readied to cause upheaval, a group of athletic officials, politicians, and boosters agreed this was happening too fast, that the departure of Texas and the other Big 12 schools would needlessly destroy a conference whose history dated back to the formation of the Big Six in 1907. The prospect of four superconferences—the Pac-16, plus sixteen-team versions of the Big Ten, ACC, and SEC—made perfect sense to outsiders such as Scott. He did what any smart businessman would: chase and acquire the most valuable asset. His hold on Texas simply wasn't strong enough.

That the Big 12 nearly died at the hands of the Pac-10 and the Big Ten was an irony not lost on those who watched Big 12 commissioner Dan Beebe nearly oversee his conference's extinction. They were the two leagues with which Beebe aligned two years earlier to torpedo SEC commissioner Mike Slive's plus-one plan. Beebe never saw that the need for diversified revenue streams was paramount to stopping this very sort of calamity. And only a face-saving eleventh-hour agreement promising Texas a disproportionate cut of conference revenue and the ability to build its own TV network convinced the school to turn down the Pac-10 invitation and save the Big 12—for now. Though Scott flew home without any other schools, the threat of expansion remains in part because Beebe, former Big East commissioner Mike Tranghese, and their presidents weren't wise enough to see the threat coming.

After the commissioners committed first-degree homicide on Slive's playoff presentation, Big Ten commissioner Jim Delany conceded that the plus-one would have succeeded. He opposed it nonetheless. Delany is unapologetic in saying his interests are what's best for the Big Ten and the Big Ten only. His business acumen revolutionized the sport. Current Big East commissioner John Marinatto has called him Gordon Gekko, who lived by an ethos: Greed is good. The only curious part: that a man so integral in building the Big Ten into a financial giant would so blithely turn down piles of money provided by a playoff.

Delany did so by following a simple Big Ten principle: The best offense is often a great defense, and he needed to protect his conference's power base. More important than raising all of college football's revenues was maintaining the revenue gap between the Big Ten and everyone else. The cause of that chasm: television contracts. Never mind that Illinois ($4.5 million), Wisconsin ($3.4 million), and Minnesota ($3.4 million) used general university funds to balance their athletic department budgets, money that would be more than covered by a playoff bounty. As long as the future of college football was tied to TV, the Big Ten's position on top of the revenue mountain was ensured.

With around 26 percent of the nation's homes in its traditional Midwest footprint, name-brand schools, and huge, passion-filled fan bases, the Big Ten can make a television deal like no other conference. Add on Delany's stroke-of-genius Big Ten Network, which garners a per-home rate of up to 70 cents a month from basic cable subscribers in the Midwest—a Big Ten tax—and the revenue gap widens.

Not even after a slew of new TV deals in 2010 and 2011 can any conference claim the one-two punch of the Big Ten's ABC/

ESPN deal—one made five years ago, no less—and the Big Ten
Network. While official figures are not released, the Big Ten hands
out more than $20 million annually per school, a number ex-
pected to grow as the Big Ten Network gains traction.

Scott nearly outdid the Big Ten with his twelve-year deal for
the Pac-12, which that will bring in an estimated $21 million a
year for the conference, a number superior to the Big Ten's over-
the-air deal but still lacking the conference-run network's revenue streams. The Big Ten will smash the standard come 2016
when its ABC/ESPN deal runs out, and the sort of multimedia
deals with Google and Apple that Scott is currently negotiating
for the Pac-12 will be ripe for the conference with the most history and biggest footprint.

Other conferences, in the meantime, are locked into longer-
term deals that in a decade could look paltry and lead to even
greater pressure for a playoff. The SEC's fifteen-year, $3 billion
deal guaranteed $17 million annually to each university, an im-
pressive sum when signed in 2009 but now a bargain compared to other deals. The ACC doubled its TV money to about
$14 million a school. Beebe tried to save his off-brand a $13
million-a-school deal that also let Texas start the Longhorn Network. Between its share of Big 12 money and its private TV
station, only Texas can compete with the big dogs in the Big Ten
monetarily.

"We felt it's better to have 100 percent of something than
just a share of it," said Texas AD DeLoss Dodds, who may have
started a trend: Big 12 foe Oklahoma and other schools across
the country are exploring the viability of doing the same.

If the plus-one ever expanded, a pile of money worth hundreds of millions of dollars would be divvied up based on who
wins actual games. And were playoff revenue to equal or exceed
television money, it would threaten the Big Ten's stranglehold on

the system that's only going to grow in half a decade. A playoff might be an on-field boon for the Big Ten. Or it might not. Either way, there would be two trails to the money, not one. And if you're Jim Delany, the last thing you want to do is risk that.

So what do you do? Find a way to stop even the most modest playoff.

For Delany, money is power, only in a bizarro way: The less money available to all, the more power stays with the Big Ten. By blocking a real postseason—and getting other leagues to foolishly oblige—the Big Ten has assured itself the biggest haul from a smaller treasure. It also means that it can pillage the Big 12, Big East, and ACC almost at will if it chooses to expand—which is why Nebraska quickly jumped and Missouri all but begged for an invitation that didn't arrive.

Along those lines, the BCS serves the Big Ten well. The at-large BCS selection process is based on the promise of ticket sales and television ratings, not necessarily on-field success. Over the past decade, the Big Ten has received the most BCS bowl bids, eighteen, two more than the SEC. That the league went 7-11 in those games hasn't slowed momentum, even as the SEC was 13-3. In each of the last five years, the Big Ten received the maximum of two teams per year and went 3-7. For the Big Ten, that means more money and more exposure than the other leagues—even if the total payout compared to a playoff is fractional. The Big East and ACC didn't receive a single at-large slot over the last decade. The BCS fits into the Big Ten's starve-the-competitors business model.

The only reason the Big 12 and Big East should've opposed Slive's plus-one plan in 2008 is because it wasn't ambitious enough. Those conferences—especially the Big East, whose entire six-year deal was worth $200 million, less than the Pac-12 and Big Ten get in one year—can never generate the league-wide television revenue to keep their members from wanting to run to the Big Ten. A real playoff, a gusher begging to be tapped, is the only way to close the money gap.

Consider the 2008–09 season, where Big 12 members Oklahoma, Texas, and Texas Tech all would've been selected for our sixteen-team playoff. If the seeds held, those teams would've combined to play nine playoff games, earning nine $25 million shares for a total of $225 million. The conference then could've written each league school an $18.75 million check just from the playoff. That year, the Big Ten, featuring playoff-bound Ohio State and Penn State competing in three games, would've earned $75 million, a per-team share of $6.8 million. The nearly $12 million more in playoff money would've evened the Big 12 with the Big Ten, negating the TV imbalance. Nebraska, in that case, no longer would've had a revenue reason to bail on the league.

Beebe, Tranghese, and their presidents never saw the plus-one for what it was: not a postseason plan but a lifeline for long-term survival. Without it, they're forever susceptible to destruction, leaving proud and successful athletic departments such as Kansas, Kansas State, Missouri, Baylor, Iowa State, Syracuse, West Virginia, Louisville, Cincinnati, Connecticut, and others dealing with threats based on demographics, economics, and geography instead of football and basketball relevance. If you're associated with one of those schools and not pushing for a playoff, you're hopelessly naïve to reality.

In that case, Beebe might be the ideal leader. Even as Delany studied expansion throughout the first half of 2010, Beebe kept publicly declaring him a trusted friend. He dismissed worries by fans that the Big Ten was covertly negotiating with Big 12 schools.

"I expect that Jim, who I have known for many, many years and trust implicitly, [will] do what he said he's going to do," Beebe said. "If and when the time comes that they're going to do anything—and if that includes any of the institutions in the Big 12—he'll let me know first."

A few hours before Nebraska announced its intention to seek membership with the Big Ten, Beebe said, Delany called him to break the news. The Big Ten and Nebraska had been talking for a month, school officials later said. *The Columbus Dispatch* printed e-mails between Ohio State president E. Gordon Gee and Delany dating back to April that discussed Gee courting Texas to join the league.

So much for Mr. Implicit Trust.

As irresponsible obstinacy goes, former Pac-10 commissioner Tom Hansen's rejoinder to Slive's plus-one plan remains a Picasso. Mere mention of the plus-one triggered Hansen's fight-or-flight reaction, and one day, against all reason, he threatened to take his ball and go home.

"It's a little annoying that my colleagues continue to float this idea as though it has merit," Hansen told Matt Hayes of *The Sporting News* prior to Slive's presentation. "If they continue to push it, and try to push us into a corner . . ."

Well, Hansen implied, the Pac-10 might have to pull out of the BCS. The mess he helped create was a worthwhile mess until it started assaulting the traditions Hansen purported to hold so dear. His posturing reeked of desperation and futility; Hansen's ideals had all the modernity of a cotton gin. Had anyone called his bluff, he would have been fired before the first SEC recruiter landed at LAX to pounce on what instantly would have become an irrelevant conference. The Pac-12 needs the prospect of being able to compete for the national championship, however screwy the system, and Hansen grossly overestimated his power if he believed USC, Oregon, and the remaining Pac-12 schools would relinquish that opportunity.

Part of the Cartel, however, embraced Hansen's brazen attitude. The threat: Keep complaining about the BCS, and we'll take the entire sport back to the old bowl system, where certain leagues had contractual tie-ins to certain bowls. "The only alternative is to return to the old bowl system that operated from 1902 until 1991," Nebraska chancellor Harvey Perlman testified to Congress in July 2009, and BCS executive director Bill Hancock repeated the same thing in January 2011.

This is like the child who threatens to run away to protest an early bedtime. Go ahead, son, and be sure to call from the end of the driveway. A return to the old bowl system would be lunacy, economic suicide too absurd to even discuss if Perlman hadn't said it on Capitol Hill and other Cartel members hadn't repeated it since.

The Cartel can take the bowl system back to the 1980s. It just can't take expenditures back to the 1980s, which makes the entire threat idle. They may have played college football in the 1980s, but they didn't pay head coaches $5 million (Texas's Mack Brown), athletic directors $4 million (Kansas' retired Lew Perkins), or defensive coordinators $1 million (USC's Monte Kiffin). They didn't have $50 million practice facilities or quarter-billion-dollar stadium renovations. In 1991, the University of Florida's athletic budget was about $24.1 million, or $37.5 million in 2010 dollars. The school approved $96.4 million for its 2010–11 budget. Even the huge sums of TV money don't make up that chasm.

In the 1980s, the Cartel didn't have thirty-five bowl games that needed subsidization. There were nineteen, and they were self-sufficient. Leagues didn't stretch across vast regions of the country, causing field hockey travel costs to spike. Schools still thought twice about dropping millions to buy out a failed coach and his staff.

The BCS is a weak, outdated system. The old one was even weaker and more outdated.

It's one thing for a sport that needs more funding to turn down hundreds of millions from a playoff. It's another to commit such a nose-cutting, face-spiting blunder as slashing revenue. Presuming the Big Ten and Pac-12 stuck with the Rose Bowl, the SEC went with the Sugar, the Big 12 linked up with the Fiesta, and the ACC married the Orange Bowl, it would be virtually impossible to create the No. 1 vs. No. 2 matchup that demands so much money. During the 1980s, a number of major independent programs (Penn State, Miami, Florida State) allowed the occasional title game to form. Today, only Notre Dame and BYU remain potential powers without a league. Pre-BCS, the top-tier bowl games often would feature one league champion against another conference's second-place team. Under current membership status, the above scenario wouldn't have produced a single No. 1 vs. No. 2 game during the BCS era.

Currently, the BCS receives $125 million a year in TV money for four games: the championship, Fiesta, Orange, and Sugar. The Rose Bowl has its own $30 million deal, which would continue relatively unabated, television executives believe. The other BCS bowls would suffer, payouts decreasing accordingly.

The four-game BCS deal is predicated on the ratings bump the championship game delivers. In 2011, the title game drew a 15.3 rating, according to the BCS website. The other three non-Rose BCS bowls averaged a 7.0. The money is in the big game and only the big game. The other bowls are simply pooled together to create stability. BCS payouts, subsequently, reach nearly

$20 million per team, even for a low-rated, non-sellout Orange or Fiesta Bowl.

The old bowl system kills the possibility of a No. 1 vs. No. 2 title game, the supposed impetus behind the BCS in the first place. There would be just three games to sell, not four. Take away the guaranteed game between Nos. 1 and 2 and television revenue dries up. A panel of current and retired television executives estimated that the contracts would drop from an average of $31 million per game to between $10 million and $15 million. With the demand for live sports programming, we'll go with the higher number. Even still, that $125 million deal would become $45 million, just 36 percent of the old money.

Without the rotating BCS title game, bowl games' ability to sell so-called season tickets vanishes. Thousands of those are package deals that require fans interested in the title game to buy seats at the regular bowl game, sometimes for multiple years. It's a trick to sell full-priced seats to a game that rarely sells out and double dip working with online ticket brokers to resell them. Season tickets are a huge source of revenue, and they're kaput without the double-hosting model providing the carrot of the title game. Another revenue stream, vamoose.

Gone, too, in that scenario are the subsidies that keep the mid- and low-tier bowl games alive. If the Fiesta Bowl can't provide enough revenue to the Big 12 for the league to handle the inevitable losses from the Insight Bowl, the Insight Bowl will die. Defunct, then, is the bowl system as we know it. Bowl executives estimate just fourteen games could survive without the BCS bailout money. With his threat, Perlman illustrated how all the members of the Cartel operate: looking out for themselves and only themselves. In the name of preserving the bowl system, Perlman threatened to kill it, without either concern or a clue about what he was actually saying.

Romantics who dream of a return to the once-glorious tradition of wall-to-wall games on New Year's Day determining an opinion-poll national champion can think again. Major bowl games would no longer compete against each other for television viewers and in an effort to secure maximum revenue would stretch the games out over a number of days. Not even the best part of the old system would remain.

Not all BCS games would fare the same, either, which ought to terrify Marinatto, the Big East commissioner. Foolishly, he casually floats the doomsday idea of the old bowl system. According to television executives, the Sugar Bowl, with its SEC ties, still could attract a $20 million TV deal. An Orange Bowl anchored by the ACC might get only $6 million annually. If so, the ACC's big payout could drop to the $4 million range. The Big East, without a tie-in, would struggle to get invited to any of the former BCS bowls. The old system would allow for just three at-large spots. The competition would include not just Notre Dame or a Mountain West power but a second- or even third-place team from the Big Ten, Big 12, Pac-12, or SEC. Bowl executives care about potential ticket sales and television ratings, not the fairness of the selection process.

The old system would decimate the Big East, eliminating its BCS calling card in recruiting and potentially bankrupting some of its athletic departments. Every conference would suffer from a regression to the 1980s, and the Big East would fare worst of all. Cincinnati went to consecutive BCS games, and its athletic department still wound up with a $24 million debt. To balance its books, Rutgers hit up students, taxpayers, and the school's general funds to cover $26.9 million in 2009, up more than 20 percent from the $22.1 million it needed in 2008, according to *USA Today*. South Florida received $14.1 million (up 9.3 percent) in university subsidies and Connecticut $14.6 million to stay afloat (up 30 percent). Without BCS money, they would need millions more. A playoff would lead to collective prosperity; a return to the old system offers widespread poverty.

Yet Jim Delany somehow found accomplices to go against their leagues' interests and block discussion of the plus-one. And it would surprise no one if Larry Scott formulated a new raid, fueled up his jet, and pointed it back at the Lone Star State to prove the superconference is the way of college football's future.

Remember, everything will be fine. Just trust them.

20 Death to the BCS

Of the myriad issues on the 2008 presidential campaign, nothing brought together Barack Obama and John McCain quite like college football. They could argue. They could debate. They could sneer. And in the end, their disdain for the BCS remained a shared value.

"Fed up with it," Obama said.

"I'm very unhappy with the BCS," McCain said.

It wasn't simply a campaign-trail issue, either. By 2010, a rural Texas Republican (Joe Barton) and a former Black Panther Democrat from Chicago (Bobby Rush) were cooperating to hold hearings and cosponsor legislation in a House subcommittee.

Meanwhile, the Department of Justice, under a Democratic administration, is considering an antitrust investigation against the BCS after Republican senator Orrin Hatch of Utah urged an inquiry.

"The notion of basic fairness is called into question by the current BCS system," Hatch said. "I believe there is value to ensuring fairness in our society whenever we can. And while life may not be fair, the moment that we stop caring that it isn't, we chip away at the American Dream."

Conservative columnist George Will declared the BCS "unfair." Democratic strategist James Carville said it was "borderline criminal."

Left and right, black and white, a virtual rainbow coalition lined up to take its whacks. Opposition to the BCS is so deep and pervasive it has solved one of the country's biggest problems: divisive politics. There's nothing like universal disgust to bridge the aisle, even in Washington.

"Bipartisanship lives," Will wrote.

Of the offended, only Carville is publicly a hardcore college football loyalist, LSU his school of choice. They are politicians, though, and they sense not just the 90 percent disapproval of the BCS but a conflict with the core values that define the country. How the Cartel runs college football isn't simply wrong.

The BCS is un-American.

It steps on the upstart. It discriminates. It dictates who plays, and if any opposition arises, the men in charge dismiss it. College football is not the land of the free and the home of the brave. It is the land of Beef 'O' Brady's and the home of BBVA Compass.

We want fairness, a level playing field, a chance. Individuals rising to fulfill unknown potential. Teams proving their sum greater than their parts. *Rocky* and *Rudy* and *Miracle* and *Hoosiers*. It's the ability to compete no matter where you come from, no matter how few believe in you. It's the magic of sports.

Too many times in our lives, the American ideal doesn't occur. There are no level playing fields in business, little fairness in government. We're desperate for it in sports because it's still possible, this place where everyone is allowed the opportunity to win fair and square. The Cartel neuters what should be a crazed November, an even more important round of conference title games, and a brilliant December- and January-worth of meaningful postseason football. Any sport without a playoff to determine its champion is hardly a sport at all.

"We have playoffs in every sport in the world except college football," South Carolina coach Steve Spurrier said. "How can we be right and everybody else wrong?"

College football is perhaps the most American pastime. It's played at the highest level in forty-one states, in cities big and small, from Los Angeles to Las Cruces, Miami to Madison. If a school wants to be great, it can overcome geography, weather, and wealth. Nebraska, home of 1.8 million people who proudly call themselves Cornhuskers, is a historic powerhouse. Iowa and West Virginia regularly field teams capable of beating anyone. Oregon hosts a pair of perennial top 25 teams. For a stretch, the hottest program in the country operated out of dusty Lubbock, Texas. Two of the last five BCS titles were won by a team from such a remote, landlocked spot in northern Florida that its stadium is nicknamed "The Swamp." And that's a term of endearment.

The romance missing in professional sports still exists in college football, and no place stokes it quite like the Rose Bowl. The stadium turned eighty-nine in 2011, and though the wear of age is undeniable, so is the atmosphere at the annual New Year's Day game. The sun crests over the San Gabriel Mountains, and the evening air tastes like a stick of sugar cane, and 100,000 people migrate to Pasadena, a city away from the bustle of Los Angeles, for the most historic football game there is. The whole thing is kissed by something divine.

"We're ingrained in America," said Mitch Dorger, the retired Rose Bowl CEO. "We've been going on for four generations. We represent something special. It's something a big part of the country looks forward to—seeing that game."

And right now, it's just a BCS game. One first played in 1902, more than thirty years before the Sugar Bowl and Orange Bowl and Sun Bowl commenced, and one with oodles of memories on top of its charm, but a game with meaning limited in scope. The marriage of the Rose Bowl and the title game of our sixteen-team playoff, on the other hand, brings the ultimate significance to the ultimate game.

Imagine: the Rose Bowl National Championship Game, an officially sanctioned, BCS-free culmination of a season unshackled from the Cartel. The proper way to dignify the most important bowl is by making it more important, and the best way to make the Rose Bowl more important is by giving it the national championship every season instead of once in four years.

"We'd love to sign up for it if we were asked to," Dorger said.

So would the other BCS bowls. Seeing as the Fiesta Bowl's CEO allegedly set up a massive campaign-contribution scheme, it's out. While the Orange Bowl enjoys longevity and location, it couldn't sell out last year's game, and Sun Life Stadium simply doesn't carry the grand setting a title game deserves. The Sugar Bowl is a worthy host, with its past, its stadium, and its reputation, though its ability to grab the top non-playoff team out of the SEC would keep it plenty relevant without a championship.

Pasadena would become college football's version of Omaha, the site of baseball's College World Series for the last sixty years. Everything would lead there, from the first games in September to the three previous playoff rounds held in campus stadiums. It would restore the sense of impermeability the Rose Bowl game held before it sold out and cemented the formation of the BCS. Nevertheless, the Rose Bowl, the place, lives on, and for history, aesthetics, and grandeur, nothing beats it.

Even an old Ohio State fan like Dorger, who grew up in Columbus at the altar of Woody Hayes, sees the allure of Pasadena hosting the national title game. No longer would the Rose Bowl be an exclusive arrangement between the Big Ten and Pac-12, so all of the great teams it missed throughout the years could now play there, and for a recognized title, no less.

"It's great to have a storied program like an Oklahoma or Texas or Alabama come out to the Rose Bowl," Dorger said, and,

barring upsets—which wouldn't be such a bad thing, really—
that would happen every year.

That's the thing about the proposed sixteen-team playoff: It
doesn't create problems; it solves them. It grows the best of the
sport while maintaining long-held traditions. It encourages
the upstart and welcomes anyone. It is, above all, fair. Lost in
the Cartel's myopia is the good of the game, the wants of the
participants, and the will of the fans, replaced by divergent
interests, self-serving arguments, inconsequential money grabs,
and petty power plays.

In a sport so grand, the leadership is so small. It's depressing
to witness up close.

A few men control everything, and if ever anyone wondered
why a cartel is dangerous, college football exhibits it. The BCS
suppresses competition and cheats a sport out of possible history-
making games. It's not just the underdogs, either. The best teams
covet the chance to take on all challengers, to knock off a nation
full of playoff foes and prove their lofty, heavyweight reputation.
The great rivalries are when the best of the best face off: Lakers–
Celtics, Yankees–Red Sox, Carolina–Duke.

The BCS supplies neither. After dismissing the small-
conference teams with a collective chuckle, the Cartel then prevents the in-crowd from enjoying a playoff ride and offers instead
one-off bowl games and pats on the back.

Well, we prefer more football to congratulatory wishes.
Like, say, LSU at Oklahoma. Or Virginia Tech traveling to Ohio
State. Both would have been first-round games last year under
our playoff, which, like the wildly popular and profitable NCAA
men's basketball tournament, provides automatic bids to the
champions of all conferences (eleven in football) and fills the rest
of the spots with at-large teams chosen by a selection committee
(another five).

Though it seems counterintuitive to invite the Sun Belt champion to a playoff that determines the national title, the presence of the underdog accomplishes plenty. First is inclusion. In every other sport, a team—any team—can start the season with a clear goal: Win every game and become champion. By offering access to anyone, all antitrust threats vanish, and the possibility of a low seed upsetting one of the nation's best teams tingles the spine. Appalachian State beating Michigan in a 2007 regular-season game still resonates. The magnitude of such a game in the postseason would be immeasurable.

Involving weaker teams actually rewards the strongest with a near-guarantee of a first-round victory, a competitive advantage three months of regular-season excellence in the making. In 2009, No. 1 Alabama would earn a game against No. 16 Troy. SEC runner-up Florida, a fifth seed, would draw No. 12 Penn State. It's a big difference, and it makes every game of the regular season—or, in this case, the SEC title game—matter.

Other options exist. The plus-one is likeliest to gain immediate traction. An eight-team playoff would thrive. Another is to cap the field at twelve and offer a first-round bye to the top four teams. All beat the BCS, though we'll take the sixteen-team field for a number of reasons.

Home-field advantage through the first three rounds of the playoffs incentivizes the regular season even more. The opportunity to play at a familiar stadium, in front of a rabid crowd, and for as long as possible would turn the chase for high seeds into an all-out November brawl. Yet the NFL playoffs prove that road teams can win: The Green Bay Packers did it three times to reach the 2011 Super Bowl, where they beat Pittsburgh at a neutral site.

Putting the playoffs on campus would energize interregional rivalries, drawing Pac-12 teams to SEC stadiums, putting powerhouses on Boise State's blue turf, and bringing weather and wild crowds back into the fray. Had all the top seeds of the 2010–11 tournament won, the second-round matchups would have unfolded as follows: Ohio State at TCU in the E. Gordon Gee Little Sisters of the Poor Bowl; Oklahoma at unbeaten Oregon, a rematch of the controversial 2006 game at Autzen Stadium; Arkansas trying to exact vengeance for an early-season loss at Auburn; and Wisconsin visiting Stanford in a power-football extravaganza. Every game is a potential classic.

It stirs the imagination of anyone who loves football, and it works brilliantly. The four playoff rounds could take place over the last two weekends of December and the first two of January, precisely the time frame of the current bowl calendar. Playoff teams would have between a two- and three-week break from the end of their seasons and the playoffs—time to heal, recharge, and study.

The first weekend would be college football's equivalent to the action-packed opening days of the men's basketball tournament, the perfect excuse to play hooky from work and permanently dent the couch cushion. The next Saturday, the winners play at the higher seed's home stadium. Same for the semifinals. And finally the championship, which in 2011 and 2012 would take place on the exact day as the BCS title game. Players would miss minimal class time. Practices, already taking place under the bowl system during finals, would not change.

Teams in the championship game would play sixteen or seventeen games. While the health of the players is imperative, the conference commissioners long ago lost any moral standing or practical credibility on it. Players practice fifteen times after the season for bowl games and for another month prior to the spring game. They play in conference title games created for the money and travel longer distances because conference expansion means more cash. They haven't followed the NFL's lead and moved kickoffs up to the 35-yard line to cut down on the most dangerous play in football. Most egregious, the Cartel extended the regular season in recent years from eleven games to twelve—a net gain of 120 teams playing an extra sixty minutes—which affects far more players than a playoff, where only eight teams would play more than under the bowl system.

Never mind that in many states a high school team, with stars playing both ways, requires sixteen-game seasons from its champions. Or that in the NFL, with fifty-three-man rosters, players participate in as many as twenty-four games from pre-season to Super Bowl.

If the Cartel worries about player safety, let it adopt the NFL's game clock, which doesn't stop after each first down. Much like how in baseball pitch count matters more than innings pitched, it isn't the number of games that causes injuries in football but the number of snaps. College games contain from 8 to 10 percent more plays (even before its prolonged overtime), making the fourteen-game college season equivalent to fifteen NFL games.

With a playoff, the health of conferences big and small would improve drastically. Tournament berths would spark interest in fringe programs. Making seasons matter more in the Mid-American Conference or Conference USA is a net positive. No longer would a team from a smaller conference have the possibility of riding weak competition directly to the championship game. Everyone, big and small, would have to earn it the way Butler did in men's basketball.

All six major conferences would receive at least one bid, allowing a league championship to matter even more in such conferences as the ACC and Big East. The race for those automatic bids would draw national interest and drive TV ratings for regular-season and conference title–game action. With five at-large bids going most years to the big six conferences, they would still represent the vast majority of teams. Notre Dame or a second Mountain West or WAC team would compete for a chance to play also, neither aided nor penalized by perception or earning power.

The selection committee would choose among flawed teams, not arbitrarily deny undefeated ones. Going by the 2010 BCS standings—a derivation of which would be one consideration for the committee, though certainly not the only one—the decision would've come down to 11-1 Boise State and 10-2 LSU. Neither team would've had a legitimate complaint. Both lost in late November with a shot at the conference title on the line. Anyway, their consolation prize is what passes for the near-apex of a season these days: a trip to one of the former BCS bowl games to play another strong opponent.

The bowls would remain in business and fill much of the December calendar with good football. They're fun events and, despite the one-sided business deals and abject money-wasting college football should've long ago addressed, there are worse fates than having them remain—as long as it's not as sites for the playoff games. The bowls' missions require teams and their fans to come and spend money for nearly a week, something that wouldn't occur with a playoff. If true to their stated goal of serving as a community-driven event that attracts out-of-town visitors to boost economic impact, bowls would stay far from the tournament.

Bowl season would continue as long as the Cartel wanted to fund it. Our panel of television executives, athletic directors, commissioners, and marketing experts says the bowls would see enough of a reduction in revenue to cause a cut in bowl payouts of perhaps 30 percent. Doomsday scenario: The current

$275 million that bowls pay to schools will be halved to $137.5 million—still enough to cover the bowls' costs and turn a small profit while the sport bathes in playoff cash.

In the end, money—and who keeps the majority of it—drives the Cartel's actions. And how it can see the unbalanced budgets and taxpayer- and student-funded subsidies and not immediately gravitate toward a playoff suggests the worst sort of selfishness.

Our panel of television executives, current and retired, predicted a sixteen-team playoff would fetch as much as $600 million, although we'll take a more conservative estimate of $450 million. Considering Fox paid a reported $25 million per year for the Big Ten championship game, that's extremely reasonable. "This becomes a major, major television property," one executive said. "The title game alone is a $100 million property."

Then there are tickets, which, unlike with bowl games, would sell out in seconds—no visiting-school guarantee necessary. Using 2010 as a model, and including a title game at the Rose Bowl, the playoff would have approximately 1.04 million tickets to sell—and in 2009, it would have been 1.2 million. Athletic administrators who studied our plan say the average price would be as high as $200 a seat, although a more conservative $150 would still net the playoff between $150 million and $200 million, depending on the year.

Marketing—from title sponsors to on-field advertisements—would add at least $120 million, according to Glenn Wong, an expert on college athletics and former dean of the University of Massachusetts School of Sports Management. And this doesn't address the ancillary money. Schools that host games would see parking, concessions, and stadium signage worth millions fall into their laps. Every school could charge boosters and season-ticket holders a premium for the right to purchase coveted play-off tickets for home games and even more coveted travel packages and tickets for road games. It wouldn't matter if a team makes the playoffs. Just the hope would increase donations.

Using conservative estimates on television, tickets, and marketing, a sixteen-team playoff would gross $750 million. Its popularity would unquestionably grow, and nearly every expert surveyed said a playoff's revenues could exceed $1 billion within five years, if not sooner.

The $750 million alone is an obscene sum for college sports, challenging even the men's basketball tournament. The money would be divided simply: Every time a team plays a game, its conference gets one share. With fifteen games, the booty is cut thirty ways, each appearance worth $25 million. If the system wants to kick in a million or two extra for the host team to cover costs, so be it. For now, we'll stick with the round $25 million number.

Were the highest seeds to advance in the 2010–11 tournament, the SEC and Pac-10 alone would have grossed $175 million. After expenses, each likely would profit more than all of college football does in the current bowl system. The Big Ten would have earned $125 million. And for the Mid-American or Conference USA, a single slice of the $25 million share would more than fund some schools' entire football budgets.

The big six conferences would still get the overwhelming share of the money, $575 million, or 76.6 percent, in 2010–11. If hoarding more than three-quarters of the massive revenue isn't enough for the Cartel, surely it can explain itself to Congress.

Getting college football's leaders to wake up, step up, and bring the game up is, of course, the difficult part. Entrenched egos are never easy to sway. Fear of change is oxygen to the status quo. The bowl lobby has spent decades buying loyalty one bourbon at a time. Perhaps only the federal government, through the powerful Justice Department's pursuit of antitrust charges, can lessen the Cartel's grip. Or maybe it's something simpler: the confluence of fact finally rooting its way into the public domain, and that public demanding someone take action.

Education can change everything. Questions can coerce action. University presidents need to examine the situation themselves, not be led around by their conference commissioners. Shortly after he was hired, Mark Emmert, the NCAA's new president, who formerly ran the University of Washington, told *The Seattle Times* a playoff is "inevitable." Emmert since has espoused the virtues of the bowl system and trotted out the Cartel's standard "We'll help if the presidents want it" line, another transfer of culpability in a far-too-long line of them. A better understanding of the current wrong and potential right can cause momentum to shift and defenders of the system to shrivel. Fans, administrators, media, and presidents—all of whom have been force-fed conventional wisdom and unchallenged mistruths—must focus on what's real.

Upon his hiring as a media consultant for the Cartel, Ari Fleischer declared that for far too long playoff advocates haven't been forced to explain their alternative plan. Fleischer had it confused. The disorganization of the playoff crowd was the best thing to happen to the BCS.

It's the Cartel that for far too long had it easy, living off decades-old talking points built on false premises—their economics unsound, their antiquated system useless in a modern world they can't change, their bowl scheme bleeding schools dry while middlemen cash checks.

When presidents see what's really going on, and when the media learn the particulars of the system, and when fans clear the smoke screens, and when everyone collectively ignores misdirection and forces the Cartel to address the reality of its racket, and when the ideals espoused by Joe Paterno supplant those of Jim Delany—that's when the BCS falls like a house of cards.

And that's when players, coaches, and fans finally will get the champion they deserve.

ACKNOWLEDGMENTS

In the course of conducting more than one hundred interviews for this book, we benefited from the perspective and patience of people throughout the world of college and professional sports. Pulling apart the Bowl Championship Series wasn't easy. Some people knew some things; others knew others. Almost no one had a firm grasp on all of the divergent and diverse interests that keep the BCS running against what's best for college football.

The experts helped us ferret out the depths of misinformation and misunderstanding. When presented with new information or perspectives, they were tremendous at unraveling not just the various scams but why they were in place. Understanding that this book may not be popular with many of the powerful (and vengeful) people in college athletics, we won't mention by name some of the most helpful to us, be they administrators, media, players, ex-players, coaches, or television executives. That includes the many who took time to read the book in various forms and offer invaluable feedback. If asked, just pretend we've never met.

Since he fears no retribution, Ivan Glasser, the world's greatest CPA and most devout Michigan Wolverines fan, was a great resource in comprehending the fine print in so many financial documents.

Our agent, Jay Mandel of William Morris Endeavor, grasped the enormous potential for this book and enthusiastically backed the project. His assistant, Daniel Hind, has a bright future in the business.

In Patrick Mulligan at Gotham we found a New York editor who recognized the frustration that college fans across the country have with the BCS. He then helped us craft the argument against it. Along with assistant Travers Johnson and publicist Beth Parker, he should be celebrated at every tailgate in America.

We owe a debt of gratitude to our bosses at Yahoo! Sports, who not only allow us to rattle the cages of influence on a daily basis but stood strongly behind this book. They include Jimmy Pitaro, Dave Morgan, Joe Lago, Jon Baum, Gerry Ahern, and Steve Henson. Colleagues such as Adrian Wojnarowski, Charles Robinson, Jason King, and Al Toby were always there to lean on.

Dan Wetzel wants to thank his parents, Mary Ellen and Paul, as well as friends Brian Murphy, Paul Tryder, Matt Tryder, Johnny Berry, Gator Anderson, Pinky Wilson, Scott "Hawkeye" Hammer, Alex "Fightin' Irish" Clark, and Dan "Gator" Strickowski. Also, Bob Bronstein of 24 Seconds in Berkley, Michigan, and Maurice Ryan of Jameson's Pub in Manhattan. Most important is Dan's beautiful wife, Jan, and young daughters, Allie and Caitlin, who deal with the chaos his career creates—in this case, spending hours poring over aging tax returns.

Josh Peter wants to thank his incomparable wife, Vanessa, and their daughter, Norah, who, like it or not, are always part of the process, whether it be editing, cheerleading, or guiding.

And Jeff Passan wants to thank his ever-amazing wife, Sara, and son, Jack, who made sure to take extra-good care of him when he was pulling all-nighters. Debbie, Rich, and Nicole Passan: You are the best family possible. To Greg Bishop, Eli Saslow,

Chico Harlan, Jon Bartner, Sonny Mazzolini, Wright Thompson, Jill Mercadante, Joe Kanakaraj, Mike Vaccaro, Kevin Kaduk, Sam Mellinger, and, of course, Otto Rieke: We appreciate your eyeballs, suggestions, and friendship.

We couldn't have written this book without all of you. We're glad we wrote it with you.

INDEX

PROPERTY OF

HIGH POINT PUBLIC LIBRARY
HIGH POINT, NORTH CAROLINA

796.33263 Wetzel c.1
Wetzel, Dan.
  Death to the BCS
          30519008864061